MAP MAKING

The Art That Became a Science

By Lloyd A. Brown

THE STORY OF MAPS

MAP MAKING
The Art That Became a Science

Map Making

The Art That Became a Science

BY

LLOYD A. BROWN

Little, Brown and Company

Boston  Toronto

Contents

To Eva Leone

MAP MAKING

The Art That Became a Science

chapter I

Why Maps Are Made

Thousands of years ago, long before people learned to write and read, they drew pictures on the walls of caves and traced them in the sands. Some of these pictures were animals that they saw around them, and some of the earliest were maps. In fact maps are one of the oldest known forms of art. They could be drawn in the sand or made with sticks and stones, and a simple map or chart was something that anyone could make and anyone could understand.

The earliest maps were simple because life itself was simple, and in the eyes of primitive man the world itself was small. Early maps showed the path through the forest to the neighboring tribe, places where game, water and salt could be found, and places where enemies lived. When people began to move their homes from place to place, the maps they made had to tell more of a story. Wandering tribes needed to know how to cross the desert without dying of thirst and how to get home after grazing their flocks for many miles during the summer months. Making war meant knowing as much as possible about your enemy — where he lived and how strong his defenses were. Commerce with other tribes and nations meant knowing still more about distance and direction. The farther away the markets the more accurate the routes to and from them had to be. And so, as world trade grew and the world it-self became larger, geographical records and pictures of the way to get from place to place were set down — after a fashion — on stone, papyrus and parchment. Few of them survived.

The maps of ancient people fell into two general groups: pictures of the whole world and maps of local areas. Which came first is a question, because on the earliest maps a picture of the village one lived in might just as well be called a map of the world, for that is exactly what it was to the person who made it — his world, a flat surface whose center could be marked with an X at the point he was standing and whose limits reached out no further than the circle of the horizon on all sides of him. As time went on, the circular horizon and the circular world expanded in direct proportion to man's ability to get from place to place, and he probably wondered, as he walked or rode, just how far he would have to travel before he reached the jumping-off place.

Even after people began to group themselves into nations instead of tribes they thought of their countries as the center of the world. Greece was the center of the world to the people who lived there, and Delphi was the center of Greece to the Delphinians. At one time or another there were as many centers of the world as there were nations.

What did the earliest maps looks like? Nobody knows exactly. They were designed primarily for travelers, soldiers and mariners, and traveling in ancient times was a dangerous business. The roads were full of highwaymen who stole every-thing they could lay their hands on, and because road maps or "travelers' pictures" had valuable information on them, they were stolen and lost.

Fire, floods and shipwrecks accounted for the loss of many more. Still others were lost because of the material they were made of. Copper, brass, silver and gold were much too valuable to waste on a map, some people thought. Stone could be built into something useful or beautiful, such as a wall or a temple. Parchment could be used for writing important words instead of making pictures of roads and cities, so that many ancient map pictures were scraped off or erased from the skins they were drawn on. Writing material was much too scarce to use for pictures.

Many of the earliest maps were purposely destroyed, sometimes by the very people who made them, because they told too much. They not only told where to go and how to go, but what one might expect to find when one got there. They were dangerous things to have around. If your neighbor was unfriendly and coveted your hidden granary or your secret supply of salt or your treasure chest full of gold, it was not wise to make a map showing him just where to look for what he wanted. So if you made such a map you guarded it carefully, and in an emergency you burned it rather than have it stolen.

For many centuries sea captains and pilots have sailed the seas in search of treasure and the spices of the Orient. Where they found them and how they charted their courses were closely guarded secrets. The charts they carried with them were weighted with lead so that they could be thrown overboard in case an enemy tried to capture them. There is an old story of a loyal Carthaginian sea captain whose ship was pursued and intercepted by a Roman squadron. Rather than let his charts be captured by the Romans, the captain ran his ship on the rocks and drowned his crew. For these and other reasons most of the earliest maps and charts have been lost forever.

From the beginning of Spanish exploration of the New World, in fact from the first voyage of Columbus in 1492, all maps and charts of the New World were deposited for safe-keeping in the archives of Seville, and only a few copies of them were made for the use of the most loyal Spanish sea captains. None of the original maps and charts made by the original explorers was allowed to be engraved and printed, so that today the important maps and charts made by Columbus, Cortes, Magellan and countless others are lost, probably forever.

The history of map making is the record of a select group of men and women who have worked hard for centuries to change a crude form of art into an exact science. They were interesting people from all walks of life. Some were learned scientists: astronomers, mathematicians, physicists and natu- ralists — men of high ideals and ability. Others were military men, local politicians, river pilots, churchmen, sea captains, and some were pirates and rascals. For the most part these people lived interesting and exciting lives, but some were very tragic. A few were swindlers who sometimes put false informa- tion on their maps to deceive others. Some held back geograph- ical information at the cost of lives, fortunes and even empires.

The mapping of the world we know today, with every coast- line, every river, lake and mountain, every town and city in its proper place, is a huge task. Great distances, straight lines that reach far over the horizon, have to be measured accurately. Broad oceans that separate continents must be measured somehow. Directions, too, must always be accurate, so that navigators of ships and planes can travel safely and surely from place to place. And all of this information and all of these accurate measurements must be made on the curved surface of a great sphere that we call the earth.

In order to understand the problem better, let us imagine a globe representing the earth's surface divided into a network of parallels of latitude and meridians of longitude spaced at intervals of one degree of arc or a 360th part of a great circle. We would then have a grid or network of 64,080 points, where a meridian line crossed a parallel, not counting the two poles as points. Actually it would not be possible to locate that many points on the surface of the earth itself, because three quarters of them would be over water. Yet even after we reduced the number by three quarters, we would still have 16,020 points located on dry land, the very smallest number we would need for an accurate framework for a map of the earth.

Study the globe and think of the difficulties of transporting men and surveying instruments to all of these points. Some of the points would fall in the middle of the desert. Others would fall on the peaks of the highest mountains. Think of the terrific cost in time and money. Then you will not be surprised to learn that two hundred years ago there were probably no more than 116 places or points on the surface of the earth that had been correctly located, places whose distance north or south of the equator (latitude) and east or west of a prime meridian (longitude) had been accurately fixed.

Now let us assume that the job of making a network of

16,020 "points" has been done. Our globe is dotted with corner posts for a map grid. The next thing we have to do is measure the lines that connect them — north, south, east and west. These lines, when measured, will average roughly fifty-eight miles to a side. Then we have thousands of parcels of land, each one containing about 3390 square miles, and each one about the size of Delaware and Rhode Island combined. These pieces of land will be entirely blank, of course, and they must be filled in with rivers and mountains, cities and towns, and other geographical information.

It took over two thousand years for men to learn how to make these measurements accurately, to find out the size of the earth and its true shape. This is the story of how the job was done and about some of the men who did it.

chapter II

The Mysterious
Earth

Cartography, the science of making maps, grew up slowly. The first and most important stage in its development took place during the last hundred years before the birth of Christ, in the city of Alexandria, the Roman capital of Egypt. Situated only twelve miles from the Canopic mouth of the Nile River, Alexandria at that time was a clearing house of information where the news of the world was sifted and weighed. Also weighed in Alexandria were the spices, ores and precious gems brought in from Upper Egypt and the heart of Africa, the fabulous produce of India and Arabia. All these were destined for resale or consumption in the greatest market place of the world.

Twenty-five years before the birth of Christ there was no better place to live than Alexandria. It was a great city, a melting pot of humanity from all corners of the earth, a meeting place of cutthroats and kings. Nature had made it beautiful, and the rich kings that had lived there all added to its beauty. It was full of beautiful buildings, great art treasures and books, and rivaled in beauty the Eternal City of Rome. Alexandria was the virtual center of the Hellenic world, a show place for

9

travelers and a haven for scholars, a place where a man could think.

Among the European travelers who crossed the Mediterranean Sea in 25 B.C. to visit the city of Alexandria was a young man named Strabo, a native of Amasia in Pontus, and an important figure in this story. Strabo was a curious visitor, and because he was well educated he was able to appreciate and understand the many things he saw. He had studied geography and philosophy under some of the great scholars of Greece, and he had traveled more than most young men of that time.

As a fitting climax to his travels, Strabo went to Alexandria, where he could explore the Nile River with his friend Aelius Gallus, Prefect of Egypt, and where he could read the great books in the royal libraries. Whether he planned at the time to write an eighteen-volume book on the geography of the world no one knows, but he went to Alexandria for a visit and stayed five years. What kind of a city did he find there?

To those approaching Alexandria from the sea, the first of its many wonders was visible on the horizon more than twenty miles out: the white marble beacon tower on the easternmost tip of land, guiding the navigator to the city. Alexandria had two beautiful harbors. The western one was called the "Harbor of Happy Return" and was used for merchant ships. The eastern or Great Harbor was the guardian of the city, where the ships and barges of the royal navy were anchored.

Strabo saw the city at the time it was most beautiful. The streets were wide enough for the biggest chariots. Many of the buildings were palaces and many were temples built by the kings and queens of Egypt in honor of their favorite gods and goddesses. Labor was cheap in Egypt. All of these things interested Strabo, but the building that interested him most was the museum which housed the royal library. It had a public walk with seats along it where students could sit and talk about astronomy and geography or anything that interested them. But all of the activities of the museum were centered around the library, and the scholars who went there to study lived in a building nearby.

The kings and queens of Egypt had a great respect for learning, and for more than two hundred years they had collected the writings of the scholars of every country in the civilized world. They brought some of these manuscripts from abroad, but many were captured when foreign ships came into the harbor. Knowledge was power, and to many an Egyptian monarch it was more precious than gold, and therefore well worth stealing, if necessary. So it was that by the time Strabo visited the Library he found there a collection of nearly a half million books in the form of parchment scrolls and tablets. These represented almost all that was known about science, history, and philosophy, knowledge that had been gathered together over a period of thousands of years.

Strabo found in the Library a great many books that would help him in writing his *Geography*. They were books that had been written many years before he was born by men that he called "the ancients," and they were books on astronomy and other branches of science. They had such titles as *The Sphere, On Nature, On the Fixed Stars, Iliad* and *Odyssey*. Strabo did not agree with all the ideas he found in these books, but he read them and made notes about them, and wrote about them in his *Geography*. Knowledge had made great progress since these old books were written, and Strabo had learned many new things from his teachers in Greece.

The books he was most interested in were the works on geography and map making, but he soon found that astronomy was an important part of these subjects, and he believed that in order to understand the size and shape of the earth mankind "must look to the vault of heaven." He also said, "It is impossible for any man, whether layman or scholar, to attain to the requisite knowledge of geography without the determination of the heavenly bodies and of the eclipses that have been observed." In these statements Strabo put his finger on the secret of map making, and we should remember that the first steps in acquiring knowledge about the earth came through the study of the heavens. Scientists long after Strabo realized this. Progress in cartography has never moved far ahead of discoveries in astronomy, and our world map today has been made possible largely because of the high degree of accuracy achieved by astronomical observers. Strabo discovered this fact in the books he read in Alexandria.

He found that mankind had been looking to the vault of heaven, as he recommended, for thousands of years before his time, but not primarily for information about the earth. The sky had been man's almanac, telling him when to sow and when to reap, when to hunt and fish, when to worship and when to sleep. The sky told him how to divide the four seasons. It divided the night from the day. Men had studied the sky for more than four thousand years, and had kept careful records of what it had to teach, so that the calendar year of three hundred and sixty-five days was noted and set down in the record of important events as early as 4241 B.C.

The sky was more than an almanac; it was the home of the gods, the keepers of the universe. No lowly human being could possibly be responsible for its marvels. For centuries, wandering tribes in Babylonia and Assyria, guarding their flocks in broad meadows, watched with awe and fear as the sun sank below the horizon and the stars came out against the black dome of the heavens. They watched them move slowly across the sky, up to the zenith and then slowly down, disappearing finally below the horizon on the other side. This was not all. Some of the larger stars seemed to move independently, cutting diagonally across the path of the moving heavens. Frequently a shooting star or comet would come streaking down the sky, leaving behind it a trail of fire that threatened to destroy or engulf the earth.

More terrifying than any of this was the great circle of cold light that moved periodically across the sky, far bigger than any of the stars and with a path of its own. It came and went in cycles. The first night it would appear as a mere crescent of light with a faint shadow of a disk. The next night the crescent would be a little larger and the shadow smaller until finally, no less than twelve times a year, it arose a fiery ball, shrinking in size and turning golden as it mounted the heavens. This wonder of wonders must be a sign from one of the gods; perhaps Nannar "the illuminer," or En-Zu, "lord of wisdom." But regardless of what god was responsible for such a glorious display of power, it was clear to everyone that the heavens should be studied and the will of the gods obeyed.

Once ancient man had decided that the heavenly bodies were the rulers and guardians of the universe, he gave the job of studying them to the temple priests. Their task was to study and interpret them so that the wrath of the gods might be known and disaster prevented. And in turn, if the priests were able to predict far in advance the eclipses of the sun and moon, they themselves would become more important in the community. For these reasons the priests worked hard, and over the course of centuries they gathered together an amazing amount of information about the universe and the nature of the earth.

Even without clocks and the delicate instruments astronomers use today, the priests of Babylonia and Assyria made wonderful discoveries in the sky. They found the planets and named them after local gods. Jupiter became associated with Marduk, patron god of the ancient city of Babylonia. Venus was associated with Ishtar, the goddess who watched over all living things. When she was angry the crops failed and living things died. When she was pleased the harvest was bountiful. Mercury was Nebo "the proclaimer," god of wisdom, who watched over people who wrote words for others to read. Mars became Nergal, the "raging king" or "the burner." He was responsible for the custody of the nether regions and the rule of the dead. Out of all these studies came the constellations.

The moon received special study by the priests of Babylonia and Assyria. They plotted its exact position in the heavens, the position of the horns, the halo that is visible when the moon is new, and the ring or "stall" around it when it is full. And because the eclipses were the most important messages from the gods, they were carefully plotted and timed. So, by studying the gods, the priests learned much about the relationship between the earth and the sun, as well as the moon.

All this information was handed down from generation to generation by the guardians of the temple, and every year new facts were added to the record. For example, the priests noted that the planet Venus returns to the same point in the sky in almost 8 years. The planet Mercury does the same thing, but only once in 46 years. Saturn takes 59 years, while Mars takes 79 and Jupiter takes 83. All of these facts mean that the records were kept without fail from year to year over long periods of time and that the people who kept them realized how important they were.

Strabo found out that about 640 B.C. some of this valuable information about the heavenly bodies had been carried by scholars from Babylonia and Assyria into Greece, and that the writings of the priests of these countries, as well as of Egypt, had been studied and improved upon. Knowledge on all kinds of things had traveled between Europe and Asia, but far in front of all other fields of learning was the record of the astronomers and priests. Few people knew how important this record was going to be in the field of geography and in the task of mapping the world.

Even though some of the Greek philosophers did not see the connection between astronomy and a better knowledge of the world, they nevertheless spent a great deal of time thinking about the universe and the earth itself. What was its shape?

How big was it? How was it related to the other planets in the heavens? These were questions that many men had tried to answer, and most of them did not agree with one another. Strabo studied the writings of some of these philosophers, and tried to decide which of them a person could believe. He also read the works of the Greek poet Homer, and decided that here was the real founder of geography. In the *Odyssey* and *Iliad*, Strabo found what he thought was the writing of a man who had traveled to the farthest corners of the inhabited world and knew a lot about it. Strabo read him carefully.

The earth, according to Homer, was a flat disk surrounded by a constantly moving ocean river, Oceanus. Resting on the rim of the earth was the high vault of heaven, an inverted hemisphere. The skies were propped up by a series of tall pillars which nobody could see, and the god Atlas took care to see that they were always strong. Some writers said that Atlas carried the dome of the heavens on his shoulders to make sure that it would not cave in.

According to Homer the Titan sun god Hyperion rose daily "from the deep stream of gently flowing Oceanus," and every night sank beneath the waves, "drawing black night over earth, the grain-giver." There were those who, venturing far out to sea, had heard the hissing roar as the fiery ball of the sun plunged beneath the waves. But no one, including Homer, knew exactly where Hyperion came from, where he went, or how he got dried out at night. The stars did the same thing, crossing the heavens after having bathed in Oceanus. That is, all except the Bear (Big Dipper). "She alone," wrote Homer, "hath no part in the baths of Oceanus." Strabo was pleased that Homer knew about other star groups besides the Bear, and that he wrote about "the late-setting Boötes" and the Pleiades, the Hyades and the mighty Orion. Homer also mentioned Sirius.

There were four different winds in Homer's world. Boreas, the north wind, blew from Thrace, a wind that rolled up mighty waves. Notus, the south wind, was a stormy petrel bringing with it sudden squalls, and for this reason it was dangerous to navigators. Some people said that Zephyrus, the west wind, also brought storms, but Homer thought not. He knew the west, and he said that in that region the climate was temperate. In the west were the Elysian Fields, and the ends of the earth. "No snow is there," he wrote, "nor yet great storm; but always Oceanus sendeth forth the breezes of the clear-blowing Zephyrus." Homer had very little to say about Eurus, the east wind.

Oceanus, the great ocean river, according to Homer, ebbed and flowed, a gentle swell going nowhere in particular. There was no inner and outer sea in Homer's book, that is, the ocean and the Mediterranean Sea. They were all part of the same body of water. Strabo agreed with Homer that the limits of the inhabited world were washed by the sea, because, he reasoned, our senses tell us so; for no matter in which direction man had traveled, he had always found the sea. And those who had tried to sail around it had turned back only because they were afraid and lonely.

Next Strabo turned to the Greek philosophers to see what they had to say about the earth. He studied the writings of Thales of Miletus (Palatia), and other scholars who lived and

Europ

Mediterr

According to one early philosopher, the earth was a flat rectangle, buoyed up and cushioned in the sky by compressed air that blew from beneath it.

worked in Miletus about 600 B.C. These men had thought a great deal about the earth, but they did not all agree about its size and shape or its place in the universe. One of them believed the earth was shaped like a cylinder and that it was suspended in the heavens. The habitable part of it was a flat disk, and the center of the disk was the Aegean Sea, a part of the great river Oceanus.

Another Greek philosopher wrote that the earth, instead of being a cylinder, was a rectangle, buoyed up and cushioned in the sky by compressed air. He also believed that the heavenly bodies were carried around the fixed earth at a great distance, and supported, like the earth, by atmospheric pressure. He explained the sun's disappearance at night by saying that the light of its rays was hidden by a high range of mountains far away. For years after, many people agreed with him.

These were some of the more popular ideas about the earth, and today they seem very funny. But at the time, they did not seem any more so than the present ideas we have about the earth: a ball spinning on its axis at the rate of more than a thousand miles an hour and tearing through space at the rate of eighteen and a half miles per second in an elliptical orbit around a stationary sun — facts that today we all accept without a smile.

The first approach to the truth about the shape of the earth came from Pythagoras the Greek, who founded a school of philosophy in Crotona about 523 B.C. Pythagoras had a great many theories about the universe and how it operated. Perhaps his most important theory was that the earth, instead of being flat or disk-shaped, was spherical. How he decided this, no one knows. Some of his followers agreed with him, and explained their feelings by saying that the earth is a sphere because the sphere is the most beautiful of solid figures. But other writers think that Pythagoras had better reasons for thinking as he did, and that he was actually an astronomer who studied the stars and understood what they told him about the earth.

Aristotle, a later philosopher, was quite sure the earth was a sphere. He gave several reasons for thinking so. Some of these were the ideas of a dreamer, but others were based on what any person could observe in the sky. For example, during a partial eclipse of the moon, the shadow cast by the earth is always curved, regardless of how much of the moon is eclipsed. Therefore the earth that casts the shadow must be a sphere. His second point was one that later proved valuable in the growth of cartography. He pointed out that certain stars which are above the horizon in Egypt and Cyprus cannot be seen in the skies further north. And because a traveler did not have to go very far north to notice this difference in the stars, it meant that the surface of the earth was curved, that the earth itself was a sphere, and not such a big sphere at that.

Even if people had not noticed any of these things, most of them had certainly stood on the shore and watched the ships come in from far away. First they seemed to be tiny dots on the horizon. Then, as they sailed in towards the land, the masts seemed to rise out of the water, and finally the whole shape of the vessels could be seen. And it was the same when they sailed away towards the horizon. Slowly but surely they sank down and down over the horizon until they were completely out of sight. This simple demonstration should have been enough to convince even the most doubtful persons that the earth was a sphere, but it was not.

It took a while for people to accept the idea of a spherical earth, but as soon as they did they began to wonder how big it was. Many people, including the philosophers, took a guess. "I believe," said one of them, "that the earth is very large and that we who dwell between the Pillars of Hercules [Gibraltar] and the river Phasis live in a small part of it around the border of the sea, like ants or frogs around a pond, and that many other people live in many other such regions." Aristotle was convinced that the earth was not so very big, and he said that the mathematicians of his time estimated that it was about 40,000 miles around. Archimedes, another great philosopher, thought that it was about 30,000 miles instead.

If the earth was really shaped like a sphere, then the problem of measuring it was not too big to solve, because the geographers had help. Mathematicians had learned many things about a circle and a sphere. They had long ago divided the circle into 360 parts, or degrees, making that many pie-shaped pieces to work with. And thanks to the stargazers who had sat and watched and dreamed, a great deal was known about those mysterious stars in the sky, as well as the sun. Many of the stars had been given names and their behavior was thoroughly understood. And so the earth was measured with no more help than the sun, a star, an angle and a little simple arithmetic.

The man who thought up the scheme of measuring the earth was born in 276 B.C. His name was Eratosthenes, and he lived in Cyrene. He was an outstanding scholar and a scientist, who had studied hard. He became librarian of the Alex-

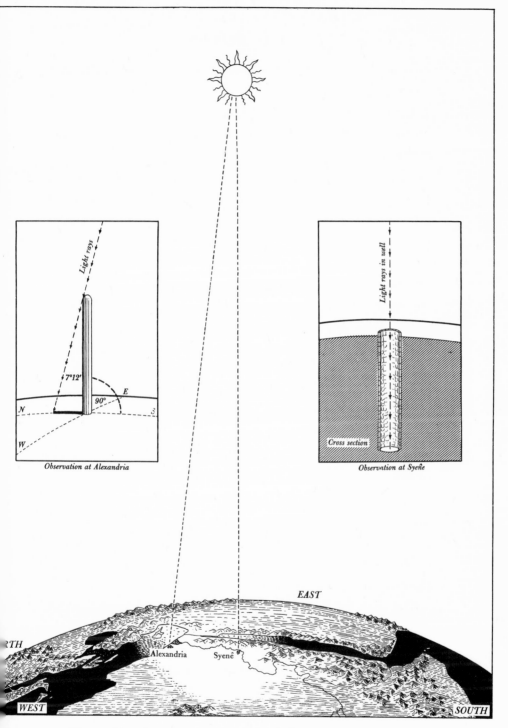

The earliest known measurement of the earth's circumference was made by Eratosthenes about 240 B.C. His calculations were based on (1) the angular height of the sun and (2) the linear distance between Alexandria and Syene.

andrian library and wrote many important books that have since been lost. But his idea for measuring the earth was not lost, and it was used for hundreds of years after his time.

Eratosthenes based his calculations on three known facts. First he knew that the distance between the city of Alexandria and Syene was five hundred miles. Second, he knew that these two cities were located on a north-south line. He knew this because the sun reached the meridian, the highest point in the sky, at the same time of day in both places, at least that is what people said. Third, he knew that in Syene, on the day of the summer solstice, when the sun had come as far north as it was going to come, it was directly overhead at midday. On that day the sundials cast no shadows in Syene, and the sun itself was reflected from the very bottom of the deepest wells.

In Alexandria things were different. On the day of the summer solstice the sun was not directly overhead, but instead it cast a shadow from a gnomon (a pole in the ground) at an angle equal to one fiftieth part of a circle. This being so, the angular distance between Alexandria and Syene was the same as one fiftieth of the distance around the circle of the earth. Therefore, if the linear distance between the two cities was 500 miles, the linear distance around the great circle of the earth would be 50 times 500, or 25,000 miles. It was a simple trick but it worked, and the result was close to the truth. The mistakes in the figures were not the fault of Eratosthenes. They were caused by faulty information and facts about the earth that he did not know. One of these facts was that the earth is not a perfect sphere.

24

Other philosophers used the same method of measuring the earth but with slight differences. One of these men, Poseidonius, took the distance between Alexandria and Rhodes as his base line, and instead of the angular height of the sun, used the bright star Cano-

pus to figure his angle. At the time Strabo was writing his *Geography,* the circumference of the earth varied from 18,000 miles to 25,000, depending on the man who did the measuring. However, Strabo reported them all and talked about them, and if it were not for him and his attention to detail,

The earliest known map (top), found at Nuzi near Kirkuk, dates from the dynasty of Sargon of Akkad, about 3800 B.C. The Babylonian tablet (below) is a ground plan dating from the sixth or seventh century B.C.

we would not know about these early efforts to measure the earth.

The earliest samples of map making come from Babylonia, where a survey of real estate for the purpose of taxing land was made during the reign of Sargon of Akkad, about 3800 B.C. And there are clay tablets in the British Museum which contain the notes of a land surveyor. One of these is a crude picture of lower Babylonia encircled by a "salt water river," or Oceanus. And there is a record dating back to about 1250 B.C., which says that the inhabitants of Colchis, an ancient city, preserved as heirlooms certain graven wooden tablets on which land, sea, roads and towns were accurately set down. There are several other specimens of early maps and plans made a thousand years before Anaximander, whom the Greeks honored for many years as the inventor of map making.

The earliest globes representing the world have been lost, probably because they were made of silver, gold and glass. They were made at just about the time men decided the earth was a sphere, and they were written about and described. But even so, there was not very much geography to talk about, because few people had traveled far. Still fewer knew how to fill in places and their relation to other places. In fact, in Strabo's day few people could point to a map or globe and say, "This is my land and this is my country." Only a few learned men, such as Strabo, could give a name to the countries bordering the Mediterranean Sea, and the limits of the inhabited part of the world were largely a mystery.

chapter III

The World
in the Sun

If the earth were really a sphere and anywhere near as large as some men said it was, then the philosophers and astronomers, the geographers and geometers, were faced with several interesting questions. How much of the earth could be lived in and how much of it was actually inhabited? Certainly not all of it. There were rumors of far-off countries out beyond the Pillars of Hercules, below the mysterious Island of the Fugitive Egyptians and in the farthest regions of the Far East. No one had seen them, of course, but most people believed in them. If these countries really existed, how far were they from the civilized world and how could map makers divide that part of the world which was habitable from that which would not support life? And how could the spherical earth be divided and classified in an orderly manner when there were so few landmarks to go by? The map makers were puzzled.

One geographer made a start by drawing across his map of the world a line that he thought would run from east to west, from one end of the habitable world to the other. It was a line from the Pillars of Hercules at the Strait of Gibraltar to the Eastern Ocean — a body of water that was talked about but never seen. And after looking at the line Strabo decided that no writer before him knew how far to the west the Pillars of Hercules were located. The partitioning of the earth, then, was not going to be an easy task, and in their search for a way of keeping a line on the map headed in the proper direction, geographers again turned to the heavens for help, and especially to the sun.

The sun gave to map makers and their map of the world the first three "natural" lines of partition: the equator, the Tropic of Cancer to the north of it, and the Tropic of Capricorn to the south of it. From these lines came the term "parallel," for that is exactly what they were: lines parallel to one another.

The basic facts about the sun's behavior came from the common man — the shepherd and the farmer, the fisherman and the camel driver of primitive civilization. Like all living things, he needed the sun to warm him, but he also needed its heat to support him, to make grass grow and grain. He knew the sun as the giver and supporter of life, and was vitally interested in its habits long before the priests of Babylonia and Assyria took over the supervision of the calendar and the study of eclipses. He studied it before he worshiped it.

He knew much more about it than the fact that every morning it rose in one part of the heavens and at night disappeared on the opposite side. It did not always rise and set in the same place. At certain times of the year it rose late and set early; at other times it rose early and set late. He noticed that the arc it described across the heavens varied from day to day and from month to month. This was important, because every change in the height of the sun brought a change in season.

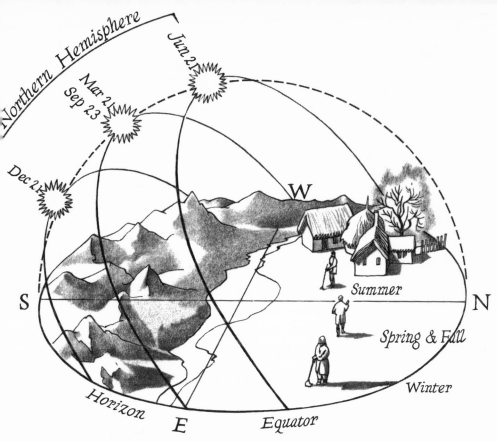

The sun's behavior from day to day and from year to year was known to primitive man. He marked the days of the equinoxes and solstices by the shadow cast on the ground.

Not only the length of the day and night but the hotness of the day and the coldness of the night were affected.

These changes corresponded with the growing cycle of plant life and the fertility of animals. The day the sun reached the lowest point in the heavens, when the night was longest and the hours of sunshine were too few to warm a body, there was rejoicing, even in the discomfort of the day or hour, because tomorrow there would be just a little more warmth and the night would not be quite so long, though it might be just as cold. So people rejoiced, and long before the birth of the Christ

child the winter solstice (December 21) was a time of celebration. Why? Because the sun was coming back.

Three months later, by the time the sun had reached the
halfway mark in its climb up the heavens, when day and night
were of equal length (the equinox), there was further cause
for celebration. Not only the earth, but life itself was being
replenished and warmed. At the other extreme, the longest day
of the year, when the sun had reached its full height in the
heavens, was also a time of great rejoicing in some parts of
the world. For many people it was harvest time, but for others
it was only a time to keep indoors during the middle of the day.
In general, the summer solstice (June 21) was the climax of
all good things which the sun or the sun god Shamash had to
bestow on mortal man. Soon the autumnal equinox would come
again and the earth would begin to die.

It did not take a priest to prophesy these things. They were
common knowledge, even though the exact days of these seasonal changes might not have been known. But ancient people
kept careful records of a sort and planted stone markers to help
them keep track of the important changes in the seasons. They
told them when it was time to celebrate and when to mourn.
The priests of Egypt and Chaldea went a step further in pinning down the days of seasonal change. They developed a
sundial and a gnomon that had all kinds of calculations worked
out along its base. With these tools they brought the heavens
down to earth, in a way, and put the first three important lines
on the map of the world: the equator and the two tropics.

In its simplest form the gnomon was nothing more than a
shepherd's staff, a tent stake stuck in the ground, or any other

kind of rod, tree or vertical shaft which would cast a shadow in the sunlight and give the position of the sun. The direction of the shadow line told the herdsman and the moneylender how the day was going, while the length of the shadow marked the angular height of the sun and the passage of the seasons. As soon as geographers discovered how accurate the sun's shadow was and how it could be used on their maps, they marked the seasons and the hours of the day on their gnomons and made sundials that anyone could read.

The gnomon told everyone that on a certain day of the year, on the day of the equinox, the sun was directly overhead somewhere on the face of the earth. Few if any people had traveled as far south as the equator, but the astronomers said that somewhere to the south there was a line around the earth, halfway between the two poles and halfway between the two tropics, where the gnomon cast no shadow on the day of the equinox. It was an imaginary "equatorial" line that divided the earth into two equal parts, or hemispheres — north and south. The day of the equinox, when the hours of daylight and darkness were equal, occurred twice a year. To the earth's inhabitants it was the midpoint between the northern and southern limit of the sun's annual pilgrimage up and down the heavens. On the days of the equinox it rose in the east and set to the west, exactly. On those days, said the astronomers, the gnomon cast no shadow on the equinoctial line because there the sun was directly overhead.

The equinoctial line, or equator, was more than a convenient division of the earth into two equal parts. It also furnished mankind with a standard "day" that could be easily divided.

The sandglass and water clock could be graduated into twelve hours, half hours and quarter hours. On the day of the equinox, sundials were set in place so that they would keep correct time.

In Strabo's day the tropics of Capricon and Cancer were called the summer tropic and the winter tropic, which was sensible, because one marked the longest day of the year in the northern hemisphere, the summer solstice, and the other marked the shortest day of the year, when the sun was lowest in the sky, the winter solstice. No one in Greece had been as far south as the winter tropic, any more than they had been to the equator, and for the same reason. Many people believed that it was a place where there was no life. But astronomers and geographers knew the line was there, and that one day an explorer might reach it.

In time the two tropics were renamed. The summer tropic was called the Tropic of Cancer, because on the day of the summer solstice the Crab (Cancer), the fourth sign of the Zodiac, first came up over the horizon and could be seen. The winter tropic came to be called the Tropic of Capricorn, because on the day of the winter solstice the He-goat (Capricorn), the tenth sign of the Zodiac, made its first appearance on the horizon. The equator and the two tropics were three lines written on the face of the earth only by the rays of the sun and named after the stars. But they were accurate lines that could be depended on. They were parallel and they were at right angles to the poles of the earth, east-west lines that map makers could depend on as standards. The Arctic Circle and the Antarctic Circle were also fixed by astronomers and mathematicians, but their distance from the equator was for many years a mystery.

MARE IPERBOREO

HIBERNIA

OCEANO OCCIDENTALE

afmaide

d

catherides

ufant

labaia

mar di frãi

clima fettino

clima fefto

fĩi della terra

R. di nauara

lifbona

R. di porto gallo

HISPANIA

R. di ara

clima quinto

R. di granata

icui

gade

E

STRETTO DI GIBILTERRA

clima quarto

OCEANO OCCIDENTALE

iulia

MAVI

clima terzo

MAVRITANIA TINGANICA

fortunate

GETVLIA

A

clima fecondo

CIRCOI

The mythical Fortunate Islands are shown on this early map of
Western Europe just to the left of the coast of Africa. They were
never found. The "clima" listed on the left side are the principal
parallels of latitude above the equator.

Even though these circles marked the limits of two "frigid" zones, no one was sure about the temperature in either one, because no one had been there. Many scientists believed that no human being could live in the frigid zones of the earth.

Just how much of the earth would support human and animal life was a question that many people thought about. They were only sure about the temperate region they lived in. A few brave souls believed that the region between the summer tropic and the equator was habitable, but few people thought that the region between the equator and the winter tropic would support life. Most of them believed that below the equator the climate was super-heated. "It is sandy," wrote Strabo, "and produces nothing but scrub plants that are withered by the heat, for these regions have in their neighborhood no mountains against which the clouds may break and produce rain, nor indeed are they coursed by rivers. And for this reason they produce creatures with woolly hair, crumpled horns, protruding lips, and flat noses. And the fish-eaters also live in these zones." Strabo did not explain how fish-eaters could live in a region where there were no rivers and no rain to speak of.

Regardless of the zones that early geographers established for an easy division of the earth, certain facts were known about the world beyond the Mediterranean. Some of it must be too hot for human habitation, while other parts were too cold to be endured. Anyone who had lived in Upper Egypt and felt the withering heat of the midday sun knew that there must be a limit further to the south beyond which man could not survive. And if this were true, there was probably a frigid region in the northern parts of Europe and Asia, where the sun shone only a few hours each day, which was so cold that man and vegetation must perish from the cold. But in order to find out exactly what the limits of the habitable world were, men would have to explore these places where the heat and cold were extreme, and this task did not appeal to Greek philosophers. So they went on guessing about how much of the world, from north to south, could be lived in.

The habitable world, from east to west, was another question that men could only guess about. Some believed that the habitable part of the world stretched in length around the complete circle of the earth, "so that if the immensity of the sea did not prevent, we could sail from Iberia [Spain and Portugal] to India along one and the same parallel over the remainder of the circle." Strabo had a better idea, and said: "It may be that in this same temperate zone there are actually two inhabited worlds, or even more, and particularly in the vicinity of the parallel of Athens" (almost on the parallel of Richmond, Virginia). He never dreamed how right he was.

Strabo went on reading, and after gathering up all the bits of fact and fancy about the habitable part of the earth, he chose the facts that seemed to make the most sense. This habitable world of ours, he decided, was a belt of land that stretched across the face of the earth from east to west in the north temperate zone, a span of about 7800 miles, or one third of the distance around the globe. The other two thirds of the belt was filled by the sea. He also decided that the width of the habitable world, from the Cinnamon Land on the south to the Island of Thule on the north, was about 3800 miles.

35

The problem of dividing the habitable part of the earth with a series of equally spaced north-south lines that would pass through the two poles was one the early map makers could not solve, but they tried. There were very few places to work from, and the first north-south lines (meridians of longitude) were badly located and badly spaced. The sun's rays could not help them without a timekeeper, and even though astronomers knew that the solution of their problem was a method of dividing up the length of the earth, from east to west, into hours and minutes of the day, there was no engine yet invented that would mark the hours and minutes of the day with any degree of accuracy. Nor was there any way of marking the time of day in two places at once, so that the difference between them could be calculated and the longitude determined.

Regardless of all the problems they had to face, astronomers decided that the only sensible way to make a grid, or network of parallels and meridians, for a map of the world was to lay them down on the map and space them at equal distances from one another. The meridians would be great circles drawn through the two poles and cutting the equator at right angles to it. The parallels would be equally spaced and literally parallel with the equator. The distances between them could be determined by measuring the angular height of the sun at each parallel, and all men agreed that this was the only way to measure them accurately. And all agreed that the only way to locate a place on the face of the earth was to determine its latitude and its longitude.

After spending many months studying what others had written, Strabo decided that he knew what was right and what

36

was wrong about men's ideas on the subject of the earth and how it should be drawn on a map. He wrote down his ideas in his *Geography*. The habitable world, he believed, was a fan-shaped belt of land stretched across the north temperate zone, bounded on the north by the Arctic Circle and on the south by the equator. This world that people lived in was "washed on all sides by the sea and like an island." And he believed that it was possible to sail around it, from east to west. It should be mapped, of course, and the only sensible way to do the job was to make the grid that others had suggested, marking each place according to its latitude and longitude. But Strabo had another idea.

The man who wants to construct the most faithful picture of the earth, he said, "must needs make for the earth a globe like that of Crates, and lay off on it the quadrilateral, and within the quadrilateral put down the map of the inhabited world." It should be a large globe, so that the inhabited part, "being a small fraction of the globe," would be on a large enough scale to be of practical value to the person who wanted to use it. And it should be large enough so that all the important places on the earth could be drawn in, labeled and clearly understood. This globe, Strabo thought, should be no less than ten feet in diameter.

Strabo realized that it might not be possible for many people to build a ten-foot globe, so he suggested that, instead, they might lay their map off on a flat surface. But he felt that this surface should be at least seven square feet. And he warned map makers that when they came to laying off a map of the world on a flat surface there would be trouble because of

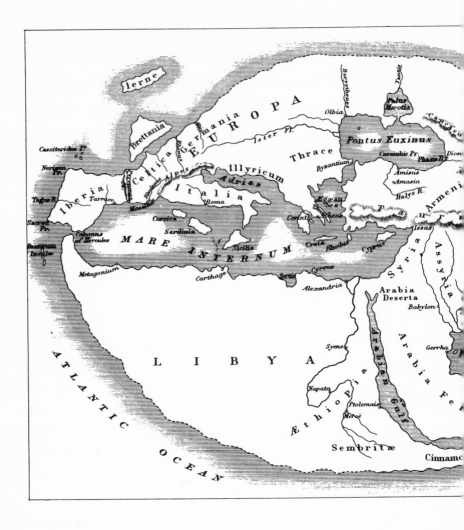

the spherical shape of the earth. It would not look the same
and might be difficult to understand. He left this problem for
other geographers and map makers to solve because he did
not know how to solve it.

Strabo finished writing his *Geography* during the first twenty

38

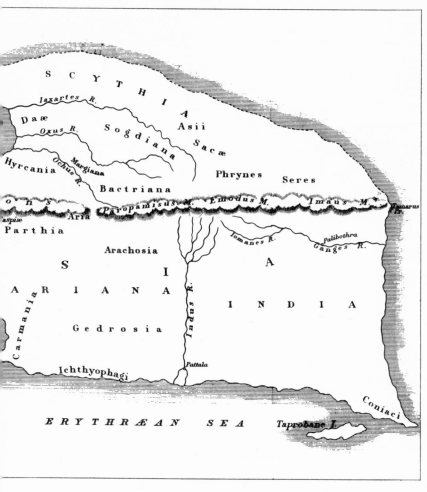

Strabo's world was drawn from travelers' reports and the writings of "the ancients." It shows all that was known about the world before the birth of Christ.

years after Christ was born. He brought together all the important writings on geography and cartography that were known and left them for others to study and debate. He had good news for map makers before he left Alexandria. Other writers of his time were learning a great many new things about the inhabited part of the world. The merchants of Alexandria were sending their fleets of ships by way of the Nile River and the Arabian Gulf as far as India, and every year people were learning more and more about that rich and mysterious country. The day was just around the corner, he thought, when men would sail still farther over the horizon and find out whether there were other strange countries that should be known about and that should be added to the map of the inhabited world. And at the same time, he wrote, scientists should continue to study "the high vault of the heavens," for in that way they would learn more about the earth they lived in.

chapter IV

Ptolemy's Rules
for Map Makers

Great caravans and merchant fleets were moving in the first twenty years of the Christian era. The habitable world of A.D. 20 was a bigger world than the one Strabo knew as a young man. Lines of communication and trade routes had lengthened and so had the hopes of man. Also moving were political and spiritual forces such as the world had never seen. No man could see ahead the long period of sleep in store for geography and the budding science of cartography. Nor could any man predict that for the most part, the geographic heritage of the human race was to rest for more than twelve hundred years in the writings of two men: Strabo and Ptolemy. Strabo would furnish the key to the past and Ptolemy a pattern for future scientists to follow.

Claudius Ptolemy, who was working and writing about A.D. 150, was a man of wide learning who had an exceptionally orderly mind and a gift for setting things down in writing so that people would understand them. He was more of a scientist than Strabo, but like all good scholars he studied the books that other men wrote, digested what they had to say, added his own thoughts on the subject, and then wrote it all down.

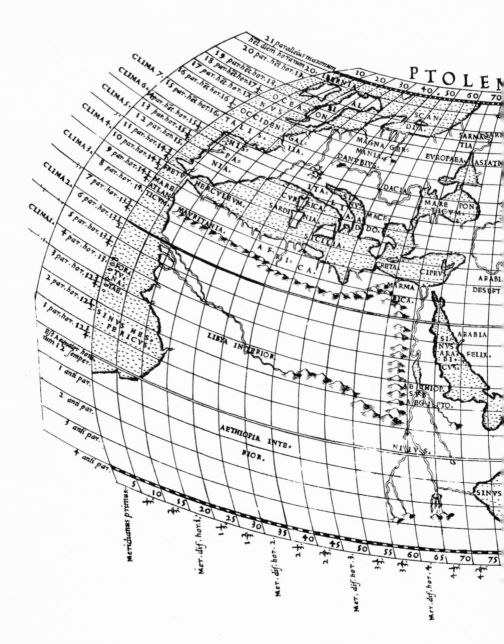

PTOLE...

CLIMA 7.
CLIMA 6.
CLIMA 5.
CLIMA 4.
CLIMA 3.
CLIMA 2.
CLIMA 1.

21 parallelus maximus
hæt diem horarum 20.
20 par. hæt hor.19.
19 panhæt hor.19.
18 panhæt hor.18.
17 par. hæt hor.17½.
16 par. hæt hor.17.
15 par. hæt hor.16½.
16 par. hæt hor.16.
13 par. hæt hor.15½.
12 par.hor.15.
11 par.hor.14½.
10 par.hor.14½.
9 par.hor.14¼.
8 par.hor.14.
7 par.hor.13¾.
6 par.hor.13½.
5 par.hor.13¼.
4 par.hor.13¼.
3 par.hor.13.
2 par.hor.12¾.
1 par.hor.12½.
Æ. equator. hor.
tum 12 semper.
1 anti par.
2 anti par.
3 anti par.
4 anti par.

OCEA
NVS
OCCIDEN.
TALIS.
GALLIA.
HISPA
NIA.
FRETVM
MARE
ATLAN
TICVM.
MAVRITANIA.
HERCVLEVM.
CORSICA.
SARDI
NIA.
AFRICA.
SICILIA.
ITA
LIA.
SINVS
A
DO.
MACE
DANYBIVS.
MAGNA GER
MANIA.
EVROPAEA
SARMA
TIA
SCAN
DIA.
ASIATI
DACIA
MARE PON
TICVM.
CRETA
CIPRVS.
ARAB
DESERT
MARMA
RICA.
ARABIA
SI
NVS
ARA
BI
CVS.
FELIX.
AE THIOP.
SVB
AEGYPTO.
LIBYA INTERIOR.
S POR
TV.
STAE.
SINVS HES
PERICVS.
AETHIOPIA INTE-
RIOR.
NILVS.
SINVS

Meridianus primus.
Mer. dif. hor.½.
Mer. dif. hor.1.
Mer. dif. hor.1½.
Mer. dif. hor.2.
Mer. dif. hor.2½.
Mer. dif. hor.3.
Mer. dif. hor.3½.
Mer. dif. hor.4.

5
10
15
20
25
30
35
40
45
50
55
60
65
70
75

10
20
30
40
50
60
70

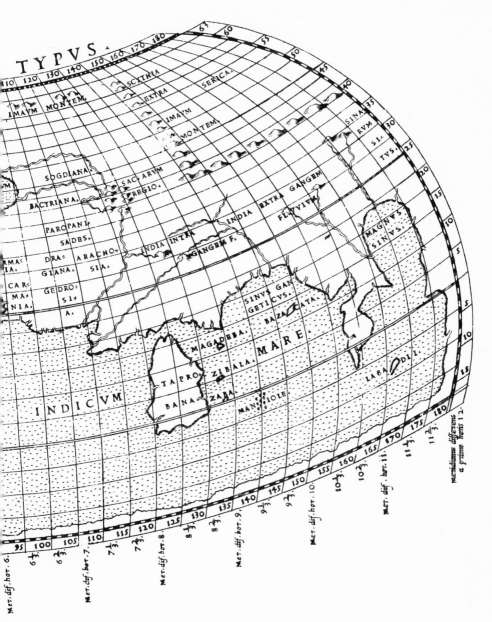

The world of Ptolemy according to a Venetian editor, 1561. Longitude is expressed in fractions of hours east of the Fortunate Islands, while latitudes are designated by the number of hours in the longest day of the year.

Ptolemy is best known to historians as a geographer and map maker, but he wrote on other subjects, such as astronomy, music, and optics — the study of light and lenses. Like Strabo he came to certain conclusions about the earth. It was certainly a sphere. If it were flat and shaped like a triangle or rectangle, the risings and settings of the heavenly bodies would take place at the same time in all parts of the earth. There is other evidence, he said. The further we travel toward the North Pole the more stars in the southern sky are hidden, while new ones appear from under the northern horizon. Again, whenever we sail toward a mountain, and no matter from which direction we approach, it looms up out of the sea, getting larger and larger until its entire height is visible. And on sailing away from it the reverse process takes place until it finally disappears below the horizon. The ocean's surface, then, must be curved. He did not believe the writers who said that the earth rotates on its own axis. That was a silly idea, even if it was an easy way of explaining the behavior of the heavenly bodies.

Like the best astronomers before him, Ptolemy decided that it was best to divide the circle, and the earth, into 360 parts or degrees. And he also divided each degree into sixty equal parts, or "minutes," and each minute of the circle into sixty equal parts, or "seconds." But then he went a step further and showed the world how to find the value of each of these parts with the aid of a table of chords. He was not the first to do it, but he did it better than earlier writers, and in a way that people could understand. He said that writers should never make an explanation difficult if it could be stated in simple words. And he felt that in order to be sure that figures and observations of the stars were accurate, experiments should be repeated many times; if necessary, over a great number of years. And this, of course, is the method used by modern science.

Both Strabo and Ptolemy wrote books which are called geographies, but they tell their stories in different ways. Strabo was interested in the location of places and, of course, the best way to make an accurate map of the world — at least the habitable part of it. But he was even more interested in mankind and his environment: his history, his customs, the crops and domestic animals he raised, and the physical features of different regions of the world. But Ptolemy's interest in geography was strictly scientific and impersonal. He was interested in the earth, all of it, not just the habitable part. He tried to fit it into the scheme of the universe where it belonged. He was interested in the relation between the earth and the sun, the earth and the moon, in things that make differences in climate. And above all, he was concerned with an accurate picture of the spherical earth in a convenient, readable form. In other words, he was interested in the map of the world, and he sat down and wrote his *Geographia* to tell people how he thought a map and globe should be made. Many of his ideas on map making are still used today.

According to Ptolemy there are two kinds of map making and two kinds of maps. The first, chorography, deals with small areas such as farms, villages, harbors, river courses — the more details the better, right down to streets and public buildings. "Its concern," he said, "is to paint a true likeness, and not merely to give exact positions and size." Chorography does not require a lot of mathematics, he said, but it does

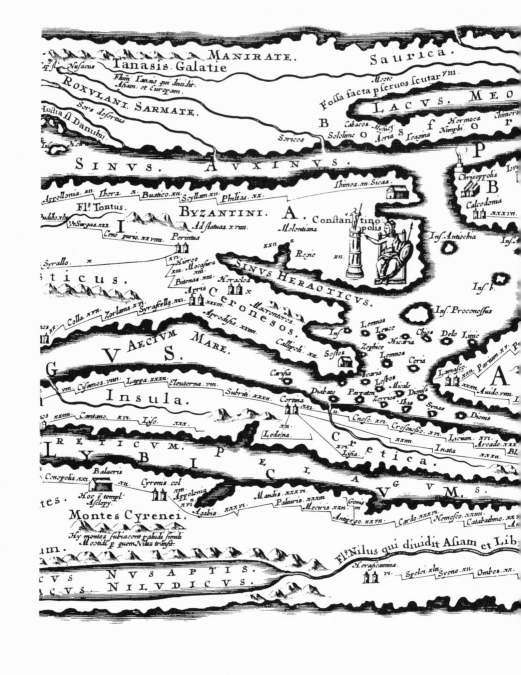

The Romans had both general and topographical maps. The map above, one of the few known specimens of Roman cartography, was drawn around A.D. 300. Though badly foreshortened, it nevertheless shows the elaborate network of roads studded with milestones that fringed the Mediterranean Sea. The above section shows the area between Crete and the mouths of the Nile.

require an artist, "and no one presents it rightly unless he is an artist."

Geography, on the other hand, should pay more attention to the bigger things, and geographers should make it their task to "show the habitable earth as a unit in itself, how it is situated and what its nature is." They should take notice of the bigger features of the earth, such as the larger towns and great cities, the mountain ranges and the principal rivers. All these things should be set down and drawn to the proper scale. Ptolemy compared the problem of the map maker to that of the painter who must first work out the outline of a figure in the correct proportion before he fills in the details of feature and form. But, said Ptolemy, the cartographer does not need to be an artist. He can set down the important features of the earth in plain lines and simple notes. But he must know as much as possible about distance and direction between places. With the aid of astronomy and mathematics, Ptolemy concluded, the earth could be mapped as accurately as the heavens.

In his *Geographia,* Ptolemy described two instruments that he had used to measure angles. Both of them were designed to help map makers. The first was an astrolabe or star-measurer. This instrument was a brass ring graduated into 360 parts. Attached to the center of the ring was a thin strip of metal that swung around the circle on a pin. This strip, or vane, was simply a pointer to mark the degrees that were being measured on the graduated rim of the circle. Ptolemy said that if the ring was mounted on a tripod or any kind of a pedestal it would be very handy to use, and if prisms or some kind of lenses were set into the vane for sighting star angles, it would

be a lot more useful than the old astrolabes that had peepholes
to sight with.

At the top of the instrument, at the point that read 360
degrees, there was a ring so that a person could hold the thing
up. Then when it was held up at the level of the eye, the 90-
degree mark on the vane would be parallel to the horizon. All
one had to do after that was sight along the vane or swinging
ruler until it was lined up with the sun or a star and then write
down the angle that it measured on the circle.

The simple astrolabe, dating from ancient times, was used
to measure any angular height. Later it was graduated into
360 parts and developed into a precision instrument with
many uses.

The second instrument Ptolemy described and recommended to astronomers and map makers was as simple as it was clever. It was nothing more than a sundial tipped on its side. This instrument, he said, could be made of a block of wood or stone

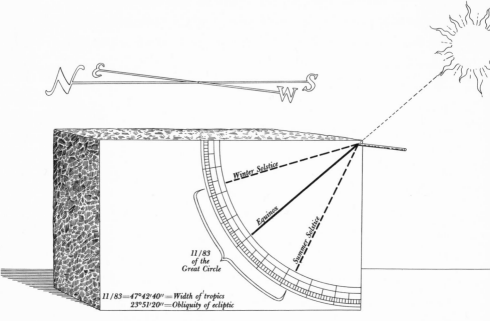

Ptolemy's stone block, with its projecting pin, measured the height of the sun at different seasons of the year.

with one side polished smooth and level. Then a pin should be mounted in the center at right angles to the surface and a graduated circle marked out around it. After that the whole thing could be tipped up on its side and the sun would cast a shadow, a fine line along the block that would mark the height of the sun, not from hour to hour, but from day to day. With this instrument people could measure for themselves the angle of the sun wherever they were standing. At the summer solstice the shadow would be at the lowest point it would ever reach on the graduated circle, and at the winter solstice it would be at the highest point. On the day of the equinox the shadow would be halfway between. All a person had to do was leave the block in place for an entire year. And, as Ptolemy pointed out, the instrument was a very handy one for finding the latitude of a place without any other help.

Ptolemy wrote on many subjects, and some of the most important things he had to say were about maps and globes and how to make them. And most of his ideas about how to make good and accurate maps are still used by map makers. Here are a few of the sensible ideas he gave to the world about map making, eighteen hundred years ago.

When a person wants to describe the location of a place on the surface of the earth he needs to tell two things about it: its latitude and longitude. Therefore writers who are describing a spot on the earth should give its latitude and longitude in the same place and at the same time, whether the book is an atlas or a geography text. The reader of such books should not have to skip back and forth looking in one place for the latitude and another place for the longitude.

Like Strabo, Claudius Ptolemy decided that there are two ways of making a portrait of the world. One is to build a globe and the other is to draw a map on a flat surface such as a sheet of parchment (or paper). Each method has its good points, and each one has things about it that cause some trouble. A globe, for example, has a shape like the earth itself, but it is not easy to draw in all the important features of the earth on its surface.

51

For if the globe is big enough to show all the important features of the earth, he said, it is bound to be too big for the eye to see all of it at once. In order to see the far side of it, either the globe or the eye must be moved.

Keeping in mind this fact, Ptolemy thought that a person who wants to make a globe should first select the size he wants. Then he should mark on it the position of the two poles, and put pins in them so that the globe will turn on its axis. The two pins or pivots should then be connected by a semicircle of metal, cut so that it lies very close to the globe but does not touch it. Next, the semicircle should be divided into 180 equal parts, beginning the numbering with zero at the equator and working outward in both directions. In the same way, the equatorial line around the globe should be divided into 360 parts or degrees, beginning at the Fortunate Islands west of the Pillars of Hercules and numbering toward the east. With this kind of an arrangement it would then be easy to "spot" every known place on the earth according to its latitude and longitude, and by rolling the globe around on its pivots, a person could find any place he wanted to. These ideas are still used by globe makers, just as they were by Claudius Ptolemy, who first described them. But today only a very few people live in houses that are big enough to hold a ten-foot globe, and map makers and publishers have been making them much smaller and more convenient to handle. Yet, on most modern globes you will find traces of Ptolemy's ideas and inventions.

Ptolemy knew that few people could afford to have a big globe around the house, even if they wanted one. But he told his readers that they could still have a picture of the world to look at and study by drawing a map on a flat surface, such as parchment. He warned people that a map of the world would not be quite as accurate as a globe, and in drawing it the map maker would have to make certain adjustments in the distances between places as well as the directions. In other words, if he stretched the globe out on a flat surface, nearly all distances and directions would be pulled out of their proper positions and the map would not be accurate.

He also said that if a map maker hoped to correct distances and directions after stretching and pulling the globe out of shape, he would have to "project" it with the help of mathematics and a great deal of patience. Ptolemy said that so few people knew how to make an accurate projection of a sphere that it would be best to keep the map simple, even if it was not as accurate as it should be. For example, the meridians of longitude could be shown as straight lines or simple curved lines, equally spaced at the equator and coming together in a point at the north and south poles. He showed his readers just how this simple map projection could be drawn, and suggested that people let the mathematicians work out a more accurate one for themselves.

Ptolemy himself made up a map of the world on twenty-seven sheets. Today we would call it an atlas. He chose the size he wanted and then divided up the earth according to the parts that were best known to him and others. It took more sheets to draw in the known places of Asia and Europe than it did for Africa. So he made ten maps of Europe, twelve of Asia and four of Africa. He used the last sheet to make a map of the entire world on a very small scale, just as modern geogra-

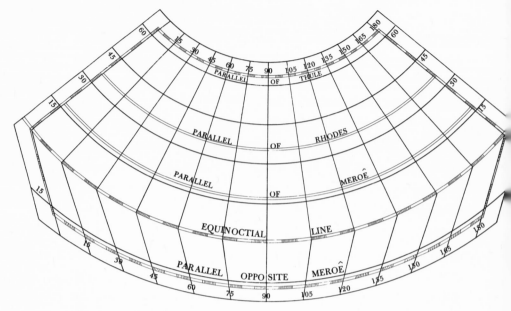

This is Ptolemy's simple conic projection of the world he knew and lived in.

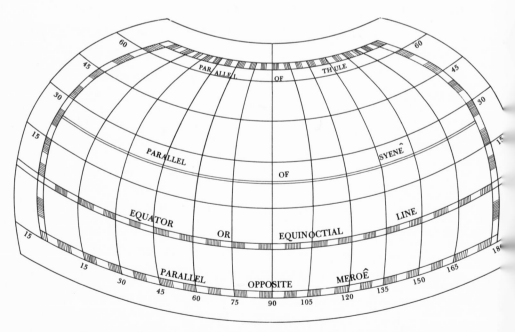

This is Ptolemy's spherical projection of his world. He warned people that it was difficult to draw.

phers do today. Then he did some other things to his atlas or *Geographia* to make it easier to use. Each map was drawn with the north at the top, because he thought people would not want to twist and turn his book first this way and then that way to read the names of places. Then he made an index of all the place names on his maps and listed them in alphabetical order so that they could be found without trouble. And beside each place name he gave its latitude and longitude, even though he knew that many of his figures were not very accurate.

Ptolemy would have been very happy if he had known how many of his ideas about the making of maps and globes were going to be used for the next two thousand years. And he would have been happy to know that his own *Geographia* was going to be printed and published by the best geographers and printers in the world, and in many different languages. But he certainly would have been unhappy if he had known that all the mistakes he made in his own atlas were going to be copied and recopied for many years by lazy people who did not even try to make the maps better and the information on them more accurate. But that is just what happened.

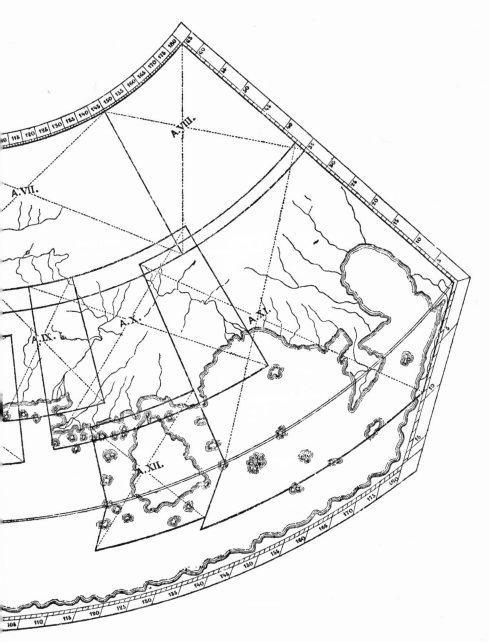

"We will make ten maps for Europe; we will make four maps for Africa; for Asia we will make twelve maps to include the whole . . ."
This map shows the coverage of Claudius Ptolemy's maps compiled about A.D. 150.

chapter X

The End of
Make-Believe

For nearly a thousand years after Ptolemy finished writing his *Geographia,* the things he had to say and the things Strabo wrote about were almost forgotten, but they were not lost. Some people were too busy to read them. Others were forbidden to read them because they were the pagan writings of men who had not been Christians, and the study of the Christian religion was the most important thing in the lives of most Europeans during the Middle Ages. The maps that were made for the first five hundred years after the birth of Christ tried to teach people about the earth and the heavens just as they were written about in the Bible.

Faith took thousands of people out of their homes and sent them across the length of Europe to the East, where they could visit the Holy Land and see with their own eyes the objects they had read about in the Bible, where they could touch the ground on which their Saviour and the Apostles had walked. Along the way they could visit the many shrines that were built between the western coast of France and the Holy Land and do penance for their sins.

It was a long way from the Atlantic Ocean to Jerusalem,

through lands filled with strange places and strange people. But the Romans had built good roads with mileposts, and there were hundreds of places where people could stay for the night. There were guidebooks and maps to tell people how to go from place to place across southern Europe. Some of the religious pilgrims walked the whole way; others rode on horses and donkeys. Those who rode could cover as much as twenty miles in a day if they were lucky. With them they carried the first "tourists' guides" of Europe.

Many of the maps that were made in the Middle Ages were based on fairy tales instead of science. They were covered with all kinds of pictures that had nothing to do with mountain ranges and rivers. They told tall tales about the parts of the earth that Europeans had never seen, and the people who saw the maps loved them. They were much more interesting than the ones that only showed lines and how to get from place to place.

One of the most popular writers on geography at that time was a man named Solinus. He wrote of people and animals and climates that he knew nothing about. But he did write a good story. He told about people in the southern part of Italy who made sacrifices to their gods by dancing barefooted over beds of hot coals. And he said that in the Black Sea region there were dolphins that were so spry that they leaped clear over the mainsails of passing ships. In the steppe region, he said, there were horse-footed men, and men with ears so long that they used them for a blanket at night. There were also people there with only one eye — just above their noses and in the middle.

In Germany, according to Solinus, were the Hercynian birds, whose feathers glowed in the dark. Also in Germany there was an animal that looked like a mule. This creature had such a long upper lip that the only way he could eat grass was to walk backwards. In Ireland, said Solinus, there were no snakes; but in one part of Italy there were huge pythons that grew fat and long by drinking the milk from the cows in the pasture. And the people of Britain were famous for their tattoos; Solinus called them "flesh embroidery."

Solinus said that the rivers around Mt. Atlas swarmed with river horses and crocodiles. The Niger River was so hot that it boiled constantly, hotter than any fire. In Africa there were hyenas with unjointed backs, whose very shadows smote fear into the hearts of dogs, so that they could not bark, let alone bite. In Libya there was a terrible creature — a cockatrice. He was a beast that crept along the ground like a crocodile on his front legs while his hindquarters were suspended aloft by two wings or lateral fins. His bite and even his breath were fatal to man. Only weasels could kill him. Then there were the dog-headed Simeans of Ethiopia, a race of men who had a dog for a king. Also in Ethiopia was a coastal tribe whose people had four eyes apiece. Along the Niger River the ants were as big as dogs. In the Land of Silk (Western China), the silk that came from there was combed off the trees where it was said to grow.

Solinus was not the only storyteller of the time, and on some of the maps of the Middle Ages there are men without noses. These were supposed to live in some part of Africa. There were others without any head at all, people whose eyes and mouths were on their chests. In India there were people with eight toes on each foot, and others with dogs' heads and claws instead of fingers, who barked instead of talking. And there were men with only one leg, but with a foot so large that it was often used for an umbrella. These were some of the fables that can be found on the maps made in the early part of the Middle Ages. They were so popular that they were printed over and over again, even after the discovery of America.

Not all of the geography and map making of the Middle Ages was nonsense, and the great writings of Strabo and Ptolemy were not burned. They were put into the libraries and monasteries scattered over Europe. There they were kept as terrible examples of how sinful people can be, and there they were read by the Church fathers who tried to explain to others how wrong those writers were, and why.

So the earth was a sphere, was it? "How can any one be so foolish," wrote one of the churchmen, "as to believe that there are men whose feet are higher than their heads, or places where things may be hanging downwards, trees growing backwards, or rain falling upwards?"

Cosmas, a monk who lived in Alexandria, found in the Bible what he thought was a proper description of the world. He took it from the words of the Apostle Paul, who wrote that the first tabernacle was a pattern of the world. And the Bible also described the building of a tabernacle. Its table was to be two cubits long and one cubit wide. To Cosmas this meant that the earth was a rectangle twice as long as it was wide. It was a flat earth with the heavens glued to it around the edges. Cosmas did not find all the information he needed in the Bible, so he had to decide some things for himself.

The earth, he wrote, is divided into two parts, and it contains four great gulfs: the Mediterranean, the Persian, the Arabian and the Caspian. There are only four great nations of the world, he said. In the east are the Indians, in the south the Ethiopes, in the west the Celts, and in the north the Scythians. This earth of ours is surrounded by a great ocean river, and out beyond it to the far east is a separate earth where Paradise and the Garden of Eden are located, as well as the headwaters of four great rivers that supply all the water for the earth we live in. These are the Indus or Ganges, the Nile, the Tigris and the Euphrates.

Cosmas found that some of the pagan writers of Greece believed in a second part of the earth other than the one we live in. It was not Paradise, but a southern hemisphere that was separated from our earth by a great ocean. But Cosmas said that this was impossible for two reasons. In the first place such an earth would be too hot to live in, and in the second place it would be uninhabited, because all the descendants of Adam landed with Noah in the Ark *in our part of the earth.*

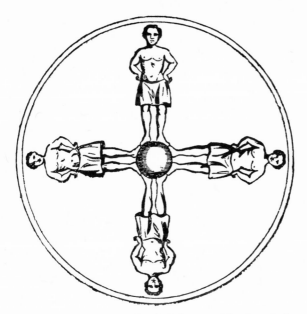

"If two men on opposite sides [of the earth] placed the soles of their feet against each other's . . . how could both of them be found standing upright?" — Cosmas, A.D. 535.

Cosmas did not believe in the idea of people living on the underside of the world. "For if two men on opposite sides placed the soles of their feet against each other's, whether they chose to stand on earth or water, on air or fire, or any kind of body, how could both of them be found standing upright?

One would certainly be found in the natural upright position, and the other, contrary to nature, head downward." Cosmas thought that such ideas were very silly. No sensible person would believe such things. Moreover, it was against the laws of nature.

Besides the rectangular map that Cosmas made, there were circular and oval maps, made about the same time. Each shape was backed up by some sentence or two in the Holy Bible. There was little choice between them so far as accuracy is concerned. On some of them the Ganges River marked the eastern extremity of the habitable world, and the Sahara Desert marked the southern limit. Many people felt that the eastern limits of the world should not be explored at all, because it would be sinful to get anywhere near the Paradise of Adam, in the "Other World" that Cosmas located in the farthest east

The world of Isidor Bishop of Seville (A.D. 57? 636), was extremely simp The T–O map at left, fro

part of the world. Nearly all geographers and map makers at that time believed that the habitable world was surrounded by the Ocean Sea that Homer wrote about. The Bible said, "Let the waters under the heaven be gathered together unto one place, and let the dry land appear: and it was so."

There was very little written about the great Ocean Sea during the Middle Ages, but some writers thought it was a narrow band of water surrounding the earth, and others thought it was very broad. But all men at this time believed that it should not be explored. Why? Because secrets of the sea belonged to Almighty God, and no mortal man should tamper with them. And besides, somewhere out in the depths of the great Ocean Sea was Paradise and the Garden of Eden. Some said that God had surrounded it by a fiery wall, just in case people should get curious and try to explore it.

is *Etymologies,* is ex-
lained by the diagram at
ie right.

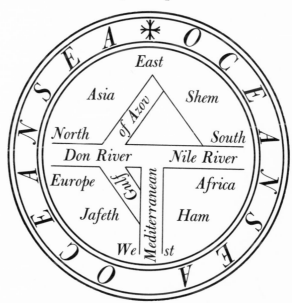

The northern limit of the habitable world was Thule, a mysterious land that some said was an island. People were a little afraid of it because it was said to be very cold around Thule, and because it was so far north that the sun behaved in a strange way. One writer said that in the summer time the setting sun, "not only at the solstice, but for many days in the year, seems to hide itself behind a little hill, so that there is no darkness to hide a man from doing what he likes, even from picking lice out of his clothes."

The circular maps of the Middle Ages were usually divided into three parts by a T-shaped partition, a T within an O.

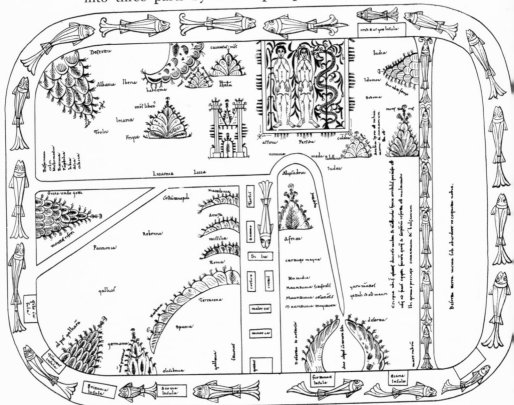

The world of Beatus, a Benedictine monk, was drawn in A.D. 787. Adam and Eve and the Garden of Eden are at the top, which is the east.

This figure made a map divided into a half (by the cross of the T) and two quarters. The half piece (east) at the top of the map was Asia; the lower left quarter was Europe, and the lower right was Africa. These divisions of the earth represented the three pieces of the earth that were given to the three sons of Noah: Shem, Japheth and Ham. Not only that, the T represented the three great rivers of the world. The upright dividing line, running east and west to the center of the world, was the Mediterranean Sea. The northern half of the cross was the Don River, and the southern half was the Nile River.

Place names on most of the T–O maps were not well located, and few of the men who chose them paid much attention to the facts that were known about the geography of the world. It was important to know the location of the Twelve Tribes of Israel, and some map makers tried to put them on the map. And it was natural that Christian map makers should decide that Jerusalem was the center of their world. Here again they were able to quote the Bible. "This is Jerusalem: I have set it in the midst of the nations and countries round about her." The Holy City appeared in the center of many of these maps, and it represented the center of the world itself. Other places, that had nothing to do with Christianity, were just put on the map, almost always in the wrong place.

The maps of the Middle Ages were always decorated in one way or another, even if the information on them was not accurate. They were painted in bright colors, with castles, churches, human figures and strange animals. The winds, that told people in what direction the map was headed, were

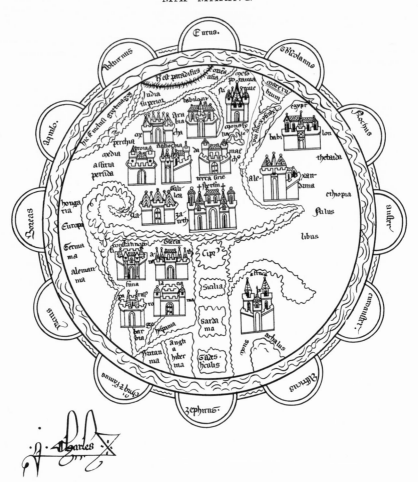

A map of the world made in the time of Charles V of
France, between 1364 and 1372. The world is surrounded
by twelve winds.

usually human heads. On one of these maps the four wind-
blowers are human figures. They are seated on Aeolus's bags
that Homer wrote about. The bags look like old-fashioned
cannon. In one hand the wind-blowers are holding trumpets or

68

horns, and with the other they are squeezing the wind out of the bags.

In Homer's *Odyssey*, Aeolus, the god and father of the winds, entertained Odysseus and gave him a fair wind to speed him on his way. He also gave him a sealed bag containing the bad winds. Odysseus sailed away with a fair wind driving his ship. But the men in his crew were curious to know what was in the sealed bag and they opened it. From then on there was trouble.

The figures or heads of the four great wind-blowers were drawn by artists and map makers for more than five hundred years. Some of them are the heads of old men and some are the faces of little cherubs. It all depended on the wind they were supposed to represent. For example, the north wind was usually the head of a cross old man who looked very unhappy, and sure enough, out of his mouth there was a gale of wind blowing. The west wind, on the other hand, was almost always the face of a cherub, and he was shown with just a gentle whisper blowing from his lips.

The religious maps that were made during the Middle Ages were mostly pretty pictures, and not maps that told much about the world that men were living in. But Christianity and the people who taught it did more to change the world and our knowledge of it than most people know.

It all began with the Crusades, that lasted from 1096 to 1270. To most Christian worshipers, the Crusades were a God-given opportunity to liberate the Holy Land from the power of infidels and unbelievers. But this time, instead of traveling across Europe as lone pilgrims, people joined armies that were

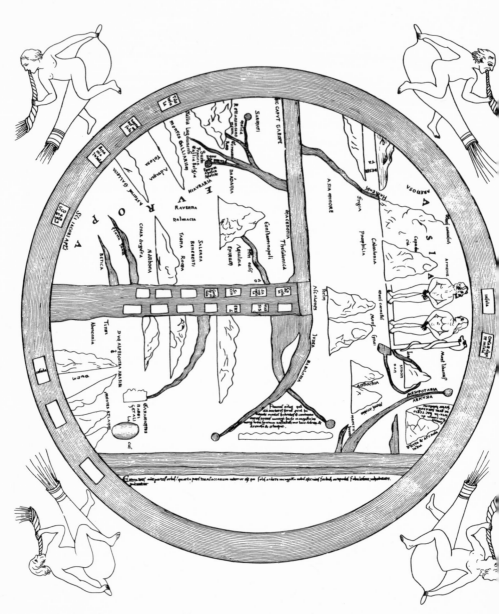

The world of 900 A.D. Paradise and Eden are in the Far East. Four wind blowers are releasing the winds of the earth from their Aeolus bags.

ready to march in battle to wipe out the people who were not Christians. And there were rumors about far-off lands in Asia where there were millions of people who needed to know about Christianity. In order to reach and teach them, men had to know where they were going and how to get there. The religious maps were not good enough.

During the Crusades hundreds of thousands of people were on the road. They had guidebooks and maps to tell them the way. They learned about the world outside their back yards and wanted to learn more, especially about the world of heathens who lived in far-off places and needed to know about Christianity. One by one the old fables about the faraway places were exploded. The brave missionaries who traveled into China, India and Central Asia to spread the gospel of Christianity brought back strange and wonderful stories, and samples of the wealth they had seen.

The merchants who visited these places brought home fine silks, gold, silver, and precious gems. Both missionaries and merchants saw and heard new things. They began to study the geography of the world, and to write history and poetry. They learned about new plants and fruits, such as sugar, lemons, apricots and melons. New ways of spinning and weaving came from the Orient, ways of making muslin and damask. They learned about gunpowder and what it would do to an enemy. They learned new words such as "tariff" and "corvette." After the Crusades, the people of Europe were never the same again.

Because all this new part of the world was so interesting, and because it was so rich, people began to forget about the

Holy Land. They read about the travels of Marco Polo, the greatest traveler of the Middle Ages. He told them for the first time about the great riches of China and the great court at Peking. He described Tibet and Burma, Japan and Java, Sumatra and Ceylon. He unrolled to the Christian world a map of the East that said nothing about the Terrestrial Paradise of Adam. But it did tell people about Siberia and the shores of the Arctic Ocean, and it told them about dog-sledges, white polar bears and reindeer. People became excited and wanted to hear more about this new part of the world.

Stories about the spices of the East Indies were as interesting to people as the tales they heard about the Orient, where the streets were said to be paved with gold and the people dressed in silk. But the problem was how to get there. The overland route to Asia and the Indies was closed to Christians, even if they had known how to travel it, and travel by way of the Mediterranean Sea and the Red Sea was dangerous and mysterious.

Even before the Crusades were over, a fleet of Genoese galleys had tried to find a water route to the East Indies. They had sailed out beyond Gibraltar, far down the west coast of Africa, far out into the "Sea of Darkness" or the "Green Sea of Gloom," as the Atlantic Ocean was called. Out there they hoped there would be a way to get around the continent of Africa to the south, but for a long time they did not find it. And almost everyone believed that the Indian Ocean was a great salt-water lake enclosed on all sides, so that ships could not enter it from the west. All the maps and charts said this was true.

72

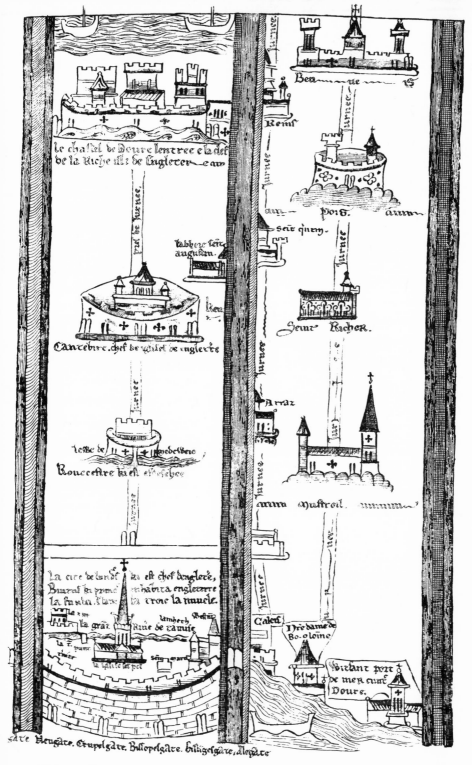

This medieval road map in two strips guided religious pilgrims from London to Jerusalem. Dover Castle (upper left) and Calais (lower right) mark the Channel crossing.

The last years of the Middle Ages were really the beginning of the greatest period of exploration the world has ever seen. And it all began because Christians wanted to spread their religion all over the world, and because merchants and kings wanted to find a way to the Indies without having to buy their spices from Genoa and Venice at a very high price.

The story of the great explorations begins in the little country of Portugal, more than a hundred and fifty years before the first important discovery was made. In the year A.D. 1317, Diniz, the "Laborer King" of Portugal, decided that his country should have a navy, and a good one. In Genoa he found the man who could build one. His name was Emmanuele di Pezagna, and he went to Portugal with the rank of Lord High Admiral. He took with him twenty of the best sea captains and navigators in all Genoa, which means twenty of the best men in the world, to teach the Portuguese how to sail ships to far-off places and win battles at sea.

In less than a hundred years Portugal had the best navy it was possible to have, and she became the strongest maritime nation in the world. All her trading with other countries was done by sea, and under Admiral Diniz and the Genoese navigators who came after him, Portuguese seamen became experts. They learned how to find their position at sea with astrolabes and other instruments, and they learned how to make accurate maps and charts.

The work of maintaining and strengthening the royal navy was carried on by Prince Henry of Portugal, and because he was so interested in navigation he was called "Henry the Navigator." He founded a school for navigators and was interested in everything that was taught there. He wanted to know more about the world beyond his doorstep and how he could bring the riches of other countries to Portugal.

Henry the Navigator was also a devout Christian, and he wanted to search out the people of the world who had not been taught about Christianity, especially those who lived down along the west coast of Africa. On that coast was a point, Cape Bojador, beyond which most navigators were afraid to sail. One writer said that south of that cape "there is no race of men nor place that can be inhabited; nor is the land less sandy than the deserts of Libya, where there is no water, no tree, no green herb — and the sea is so shallow that a whole league from land it is only a fathom [six feet] deep, while the currents are so terrible that no ship, having once passed the Cape, will ever be able to return."

Prince Henry did not believe these stories, and he wanted his captains to find out more about the Western Sea and the lands that lay to the south of Cape Bojador. So about the year 1415 he launched a series of expeditions to explore the coast of Africa, and the orders he gave his captains were to round Cape Bojador and to make charts of every new thing they discovered. The expeditions were costly, and many people laughed at Prince Henry and said he was wasting money, and that all his ships would be lost and Portugal would be ruined. But in 1434, one of his captains rounded the Cape, and the next year another one of his ships sailed fifty leagues to the south of it. Both captains came home safely with their charts and reported what they had seen and done. Seven years after the Cape was first rounded, one of Henry's captains brought back a ship — loaded with slaves and enough gold dust to convince everyone in Portugal that Henry the Navigator was right and they were wrong.

His ships explored the Madeira Islands and the Canaries. One of them discovered the Cape Verde Islands. And every captain made a chart and kept a log of what he had found and where it was located. Not only gold and slaves, but sugar from the Azores, began to come into Portugal, and the country soon became rich. More scientists were brought in from other countries to teach astronomy and navigation to the young men of Portugal. Better ships were built, and one writer says that because of Henry the Navigator and his love of the sea, Portuguese caravels at that time were the best ships afloat.

Henry the Navigator did not live to see the great climax of Portuguese explorations along the west coast of Africa. It happened twenty-eight years after his death. In August, 1487, Bartholomeu Dias sailed from Lisbon with three ships. His course was the same as usual — south, and if possible still further south. Down along the coast of Africa he sailed, south and further south, where no man had ever sailed. For thirteen days he was driven by storms and gales and for a time he was lost. After the weather had cleared up a little he set his course to the east, so that he would hit the coast of Africa at one point or another. But after sailing eastward for several days he found nothing but open water around him. The coast was not there, and his crew was beginning to be uneasy about getting home. So he turned north and finally saw ahead of him the southern coast of Cape Colony at Mossel Bay, halfway between the Cape of Good Hope and Port Elizabeth. The date was February 3, 1488. At that point he turned eastward again and came to the estuary of the Great Fish River. There he could plainly see the northeasterly trend of the coast. He knew what he had found, and it was enough. The great continent of Africa could be rounded. The Indian Ocean that had been shown on maps and charts as a great salt lake since the days of Claudius Ptolemy was open water. And an ocean route to the Spice Islands of the Indies had been found at last.

chapter VI

Charts and Roses

During the thousands of years when philosophers and dreamers were watching the stars and talking about the world and how big it was, there was another kind of fellow thinking about the same things. He was the man who sailed the seas, the sailor who stood his watch at night and the navigator who steered his ship from one port to another. These men did more than dream, because it was a matter of life and death to know where they were going and how they could get there safely and in the shortest possible time. Their charts had to be accurate and their sailing directions had to be simple and clear to read.

The men who went "down to the sea in ships" and ventured forth upon great waters had many secrets, and they did not write them down for others to read. They were secrets about how they were able to sail away from home, out beyond the sight of land, and steer their ships to another port in all kinds of weather without going on the rocks. When they learned a shorter route between two harbors they said nothing about it, and when they found a wonderful place to fish, far away from home, they kept it to themselves. Their world was the sea, and not the world of Strabo and Ptolemy.

The first chapter in the story of sea charts and navigation

goes back twelve hundred years before the birth of Christ, before Homer began to write poetry and stories about Odysseus. It is the story of the Phoenicians. Historians have learned a great deal about the Phoenicians by piecing bits of information together. They have learned about their history as a nation, their commerce and their religion. But the record of how they sailed their ships has not been found. Yet all along the coasts of the Mediterranean Sea, from one end to the other, there are traces of their colonies and their fame.

The Phoenicians were an offshoot of one of the Semitic tribes who called themselves Canaanites. The Bible says that they were descendants of Ham, one of Noah's sons. They lived in the land of Canaan, a small part of the coast of Syria. Their capital city was Tyre, which was on an island. Strabo wrote about it from the books he had read. The houses, he said, had many stories, even more than the houses in Rome. At one time Tyre had suffered from a bad earthquake that almost wiped it out, and later Alexander the Great had captured it by siege. But, according to Strabo, in spite of its troubles it grew strong and rich, "both because of the seamanship of its people, in which the Phoenicians in general have been superior to all peoples of all times, and because of their dye-houses, for the Tyrian purple has proved itself to be by far the most beautiful." Today Tyre would be called an industrial city that made cloth and dyed it "royal purple."

In spite of their important industry, the Phoenicians were first of all a seafaring nation. Their sailors were called "red men" because of their skin, which was weathered and sunburned from long days at sea. The Phoenicians knew many of

79

the "secrets of the sea," and even more important, the secrets of the heavens, but just how much they knew about navigation and astronomy we will never know. But what we do know is that they were brave and skillful. They dared to sail where others were not willing to go. And because of their skill and daring they became powerful. They filled their ships with the merchandise of other nations and took it where it was supposed to go. And when another country needed naval ships to fight a battle, the Phoenicians were ready and willing to do the job — for a price. They were hated in Greece and they were also feared.

Phoenician ships were the best afloat, and models for all the sailors who have lived since then. About five hundred years before the birth of Christ, a Greek historian described one in order to tell his readers how important it is to be orderly in small things:

> The best and most accurate arrangement of things I think I ever saw, was when I went to look at the great Phoenician ship. For I saw the greatest quantity of tackling separately disposed in the smallest stowage. You know that a ship comes to anchor and gets under way by means of many wooden instruments and many ropes, and sails by means of many sails. And it is armed with many machines to fight off hostile vessels. It carries about with it many arms for the crew, and all the apparatus which men use in a dwelling house for each meal. Besides all this, the vessel is filled with cargo which the owner carries for profit.
>
> And all that I have mentioned lay in not much greater space than would be found in a bedroom large enough conveniently to hold ten beds. All things, too, lay in such a way

that they did not interfere with one another, so that they needed no one to hunt for them. They could easily be gathered together, and there were no knots to be untied that might cause delay if they were suddenly wanted.

I found the mate of the steersman, who is called the prow's man, so well acquainted with the location of each article that even when absent he could tell where everything lay, and what their number was, just as a person who has learnt to read could tell the number and order of the letters in the name of Socrates. I saw this man examining, at an unoccupied time, everything that is of use on board a ship; and on my asking him the reason, he replied, "Stranger, I am looking to see whether anything is lacking or out of order; for it will be no time to look for what is missing or out of place when a storm comes up at sea."

This description of a Phoenician ship written more than twenty-three hundred years ago proves that their captains and pilots were able men, but it does not tell us how well or how far they were able to sail. But history does tell us, in other places, about the colonies the Phoenicians established along the coasts and islands of the Mediterranean Sea. These stories prove that the Phoenicians knew how to sail their ships as well as keep them in good order.

Some historians, who did not know much about the Phoenicians, have said that before the invention of the mariners' compass, sailors did not dare to sail out beyond the sight of land or sail at night. The history of the Phoenicians proves that this is not true. Homer wrote about them sailing the waters around Greece before his time. They sailed the length of the Adriatic and settled some of their people on the western shore

81

of the toe of Italy and the eastern coast of Sicily. They captured the island of Malta, and at one time their settlers were on the islands of Sardinia and Corsica. They occupied most of the coast of Africa from the Gulf of Sidra to Tangier. Carthage and Utica, on the Bay of Tunis, were their great trading centers.

According to Strabo, even in his day the Phoenicians occupied the most important parts of the continent of Europe facing the Mediterranean Sea. He wrote that at one time they had settled three hundred cities in Libya, and that there were seven hundred thousand Phoenicians in the city of Carthage. From Tyre and Sidon in Syria, the Phoenicians sailed their ships to the other end of the Mediterranean Sea, keeping close watch on their colonies and trading posts 2200 miles away. How did they do it without sailing outside of the sight of land? It was impossible then as it is now.

How could the Phoenicians sail the distances they did without sailing at night? The distance between the island of Malta and the port of Alexandria is 820 miles, and to Port Said, 940 miles in a straight line! Strabo helped to solve this riddle when he said that the Phoenicians were "philosophers in the sciences of astronomy and arithmetic, having begun their studies with practical arithmetic and with night-sailings." He also said that the Little Bear or Little Dipper in the heavens was not known to the Greeks until the Phoenicians told them about it and how it could be used to guide a ship at night.

The Phoenicians knew about the stars and how to steer by them. They also knew about charts and how to make them. How good their charts were, we will never know, because they were kept secret from other people and probably most of them were destroyed. The Phoenicians also had books of sailing directions that told their captains how to pilot their ships from one harbor to another, and where they could find shelter and a good anchorage. These books of sailing directions also told where to find food and water and firewood for cooking. One of these books, written about five hundred years before Christ, describes how to sail around the entire coast of the Mediterranean Sea and the Black Sea, and how many days and nights it takes to sail from one harbor to another.

From the very beginning, sea charts were one of the most important tools of the navigator, at least until the compass was invented. They did their best to tell him distances and directions. They gave him a picture of the coasts and harbors, the location of dangerous shoals and reefs and submerged rocks that might wreck his ship. Charts were not concerned with the size and shape of the earth, but only with the simple facts that would help a mariner sail where he wanted to sail.

The problem of how to describe direction was one that puzzled chart makers for a long time. To primitive people it was good enough to say that a place was "towards the darkness" when they meant towards the north, and "towards the light" when they meant towards the south. But it was no help to navigators to hear that a place was in the direction of "the summer sunrise" (east) or the "winter sunset" on the west. They needed to know exactly what direction they had to sail in order to get where they were going, and for this reason they developed a "wind rose" that they could draw on their charts, a circle with points reaching out in all directions with names for each point. They named the points after the winds and the directions from which they blew.

Every country had its favorite names for the winds that blew across it, and for many years there was great confusion. Chart-makers put wind roses on their charts, but the names of the winds were different in every country, and they were put there to help only the people at home. As time went on people began to think that it would be sensible to have a system of describing directions that anybody could understand, no matter where he lived. They tried several schemes of dividing up the circular horizon. The simplest was the wind rose that Homer wrote about, with only four winds and four directions. This was not good enough for sailors. Then they tried a wind rose with eight winds, but this was still not good enough. Finally, about the year A.D. 800, the Emperor Charlemagne and his sea captains came up with an idea for a wind rose that would be useful to navigators everywhere.

Charlemagne's wind rose had thirty-two "points" on it instead of eight or sixteen. And instead of having long names such as *Vulturnus* and *Apeliotes* that people could not spell or pronounce, the names of the winds were simple. There were only four principal winds on the rose — *Nord, Est, Sud* and *Oest*. Then instead of adding a lot of new names, the four principal winds were divided into half-winds and quarter-winds. Everybody liked the idea because it was so simple, and in time the wind rose with thirty-two points was used in all countries, and could be understood in any language. Going around the circle it read: East, East by South, East Southeast, Southeast by East, Southeast, and so on.

The modern compass is a combination of the ancient rose of

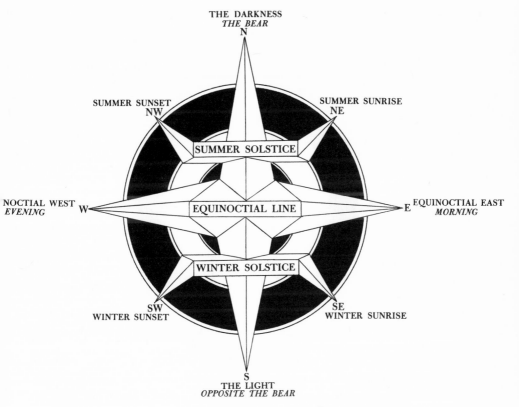

THE DARKNESS
THE BEAR
N

SUMMER SUNSET
NW

SUMMER SUNRISE
NE

SUMMER SOLSTICE

NOCTIAL WEST
EVENING
W

EQUINOCTIAL LINE

E EQUINOCTIAL EAST
MORNING

WINTER SOLSTICE

SW
WINTER SUNSET

SE
WINTER SUNRISE

S
THE LIGHT
OPPOSITE THE BEAR

This is the wind rose of the ancients, the directions that were important to them. These directions were not accurate enough for good map making.

the winds and a magnetized needle. The wind rose was just a convenient way of dividing up the circular horizon into parts of equal size, and the naming of the winds was as natural as the naming of the stars. It was also natural that the rose of the winds should be fastened to the greatest of all instruments for finding direction — the compass needle.

No one knows who invented the compass needle, but just

85

about the time Claudius Ptolemy was writing his *Geographia* other people began to write about a special kind of iron ore. It was called magnetite, and this metal did strange things to a needle. If you rubbed a needle with magnetite, or "loadstone" as some people called it, and mounted the needle so that it would swing freely, it would always point to the north and south. The Chinese knew all about it, and some believe that the Vikings used a magnetized needle fastened to a pin to guide them in strange waters. The best loadstones were found in the East Indies, on the coast of China and in Bengal. These wonderful chunks of metal would lift their own weight in iron or steel, and in Europe they were sold for their weight in silver.

During the Middle Ages a poet wrote that he wished the Heavenly Father would give to men a way of guiding their ships to a safe harbor; something that was as faithful and dependable as the polestar. And he thought perhaps the good Lord had provided something that might work almost as well, and that was the loadstone and magnetized needle. "For when the stars and the moon are hidden by storms or darkness," he wrote, "the sailor can use a little trick that does not fail to help him fix and steer his course. All he has to do is put into a bowl of water a piece of straw pierced by a needle that has been rubbed with an ugly brown stone. The point of this floating needle will always point toward the polestar." If there was no straw around, he added, a piece of cork would do just as well. Another man decided that it would be a good idea to balance the magnetized needle on a pivot or pin so that it could swing around without floating in water.

In time someone thought up the idea of fastening the old

rose of the winds with its thirty-two points to the magnetized needle and mounting the whole thing on a pivot that would swing in any direction. Today our mariners' compasses are nearly the same as they were seven or eight hundred years ago. They are nothing more than a magnetized needle fastened to a compass card that is marked off with the thirty-two "points" of the winds. Most of them float in alcohol that will not freeze as easily as water, and the whole compass is mounted in a box so that it will swing and sway in rough weather and turn itself so that the needle and the card will always point in the right direction.

Even the earliest sea charts are beautiful to look at. They were drawn or painted on parchment in bright colors. Sometimes they were decorated with silver and gold leaf. Often there was more than one reason for painting them in bright colors. In Italy the artists who made charts painted the winds, the half-winds and quarter-winds in different colors so that they would be easy to read and follow. The principal winds on the compass rose were done in gold, the half-winds in green, and the quarter-winds in red. Lines were drawn from the points of the central compass rose all the way across the chart, and these, too, were colored the same as the points on the compass rose. This made it easier for a navigator to trace a compass course from the compass rose. The north point of the compass rose was always decorated with a fleur-de-lis, just as it is today.

About the time Christopher Columbus sailed across the great Western Sea, sailors began to realize that their compasses did not point directly to the North Star. And they noticed that in different parts of the ocean and the Mediterranean Sea there was quite a difference in the way compasses behaved. In some places the compass pointed almost true north. Then again there were spots in the ocean where it pointed several degrees to either side of the North Star. They did not understand why this happened, but they corrected their compasses by fastening

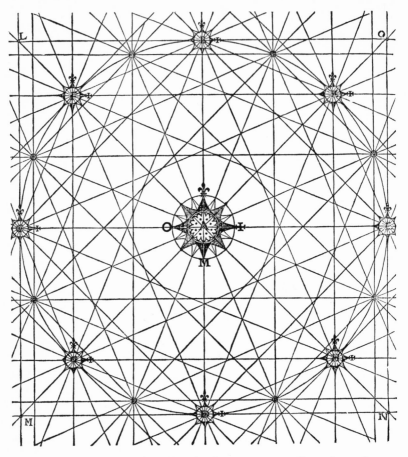

A sea chart drawn four hundred years ago and used to plot a ship's course in deep water.

the needle to one side or the other on the compass card so that on short voyages it was accurate. It was many years before people realized that there were very few places in the world where the compass would point true north, and that there was a *magnetic* North Pole on the earth as well as a *true* North Pole in the sky.

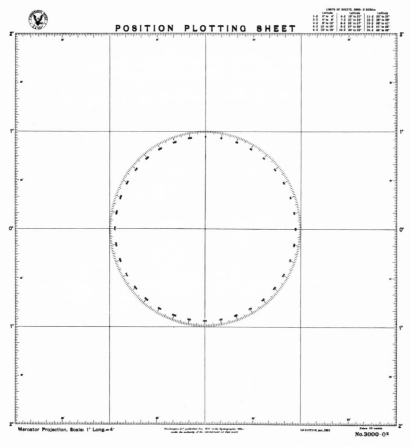

The same kind of chart, used by modern sailors, is much simpler to use, and all the arithmetic has been done.

89

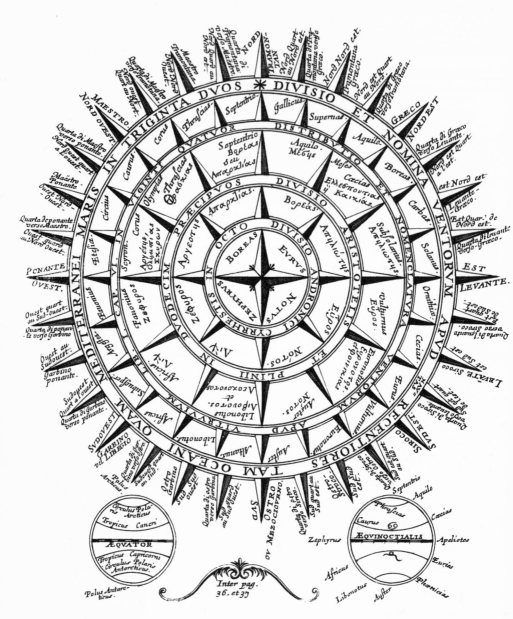

Three hundred years ago a man drew this picture of a wind rose to show all the names people had invented to describe directions. The names are in several languages.

The compass rose on sea charts was beautiful to look at, but the pretty lines that fanned out from it would not help a sailor steer his ship in the direction he wanted to go. Why? Because a straight line on a chart is not the same as a straight line on the globe of the earth, or an ocean that curves the same way as the earth. If the compass rose were pasted onto a globe, the lines fanning out from it would be curved lines wrapped around it like a spider's legs. The chart makers tried to think of a way to make a chart that would have straight lines coming from the compass rose that would give a sailor the right course to steer. This meant that they had to spread out the globe on a flat sheet of paper or parchment and see what happened.

The man who solved the riddle of how to do this was Gerhard Kremer. We know him better as Gerard Mercator. He was a map maker and he also made compasses and instruments for measuring angles, such as astrolabes. He was born in the year 1512 at Rupelmonde in East Flanders, not long after the great discoveries of Columbus. The world had to wait for him to grow up, but in the meantime everybody who sailed from Europe to the New World of America needed better charts to steer by. The Atlantic Ocean was broad and deep. No one knew how far it was to the New World from Spain and Portugal, but all navigators knew that a straight line on their charts would not take them where they wanted to go. Most navigators were satisfied to sail westward with the trade winds until some land appeared. Then if they could identify it and knew their position, they could steer either to the north or south for the harbor they wanted to anchor in.

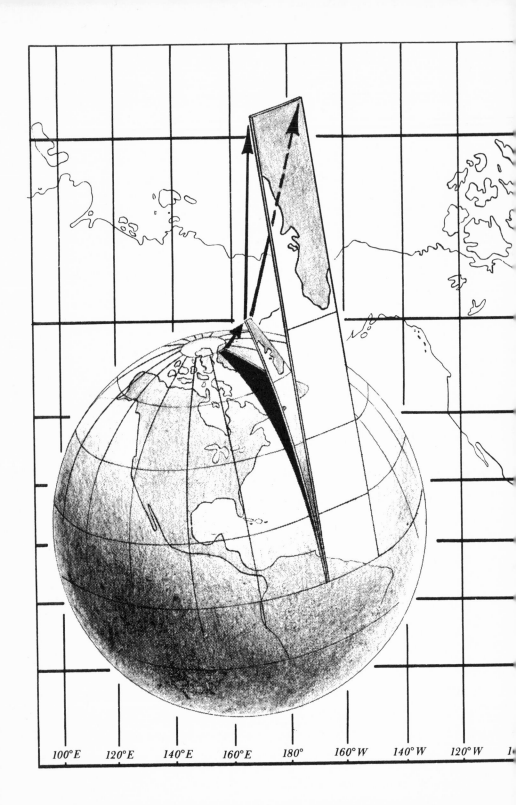

100°E 120°E 140°E 160°E 180° 160°W 140°W 120°W

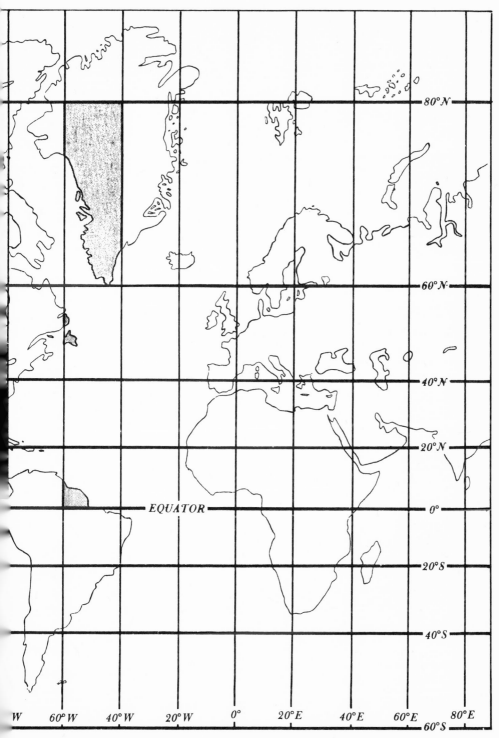

A gore of the globe peeled and projected according to the scheme
devised by Gerard Mercator. This is the projection used on modern
sailing charts.

Mercator finally grew up and settled down in Louvain. He worked with his hands as well as his brain. The instruments he made were beautiful to look at and carefully made. His globes of the earth and his charts of the heavens became famous all over Europe. He made a pair of globes for the Emperor Charles V. The celestial globe was made of crystal with the stars of the constellations etched on the surface with a diamond. Inside it was a little globe of the world made of wood. The map of the world was first drawn and painted on strips of paper called gores and then pasted to the globe. This kind of workmanship made Mercator both famous and rich.

Mercator was a scholar as well as a craftsman, and after he had been in the map-making business for thirty years he decided that what the world needed was an accurate chart, and one that was simple enough for any navigator to use and steer by. So he tackled the problem of how to straighten out the spiral lines fanning out from the compass rose on a globe and how to make them point in the right direction on a flat sheet of paper or parchment. In other words, he wanted to "project" the lines from the compass rose across the chart in such a way that straight lines on the chart would tell the same story as the curved ones on the globe. In order to do this he would have to pull and stretch the surface of the globe a great deal. He also knew that the mariners of the world did most of their sailing in the waters that lay between the two temperate zones on the earth. They were not interested in the arctic or antarctic regions. This being so, he decided to make his projection so that the parts between the temperate zones would get the least stretching on his chart.

Mercator's chart, laid out on his new projection, was engraved and published in 1569. For a time sailors were afraid to use it. They had enough troubles as it was, and they were not interested in trying to figure out how a picture of the globe could be drawn on a sheet of paper and come out so that they could lay off a compass course on it and get where they wanted to go. But after they tried the new projection for a while, they grew to like it. They liked it even better after an English scholar and scientist named Edward Wright explained to them just how it worked and how simple it was to use.

Instead of trying to scare the life out of sailors and others, Edward Wright described the Mercator projection in very simple words. He said to imagine the globe as a balloon suspended inside a cylinder or tube. Then, he said, if the balloon is blown up it will be squeezed against the sides of the tube. The more it is blown up the longer the globe will get. At the same time the meridians of longitude will be straightened out so that they will be parallel to one another. The parallels of latitude will stay parallel to one another, but they will be farther apart. But no matter how much the globe is blown up, no matter how much it is stretched, the meridians and parallels will be straight lines at right angles to one another and *directions* will not be changed.

Mercator's projection and chart did strange things to the shape of the earth's surface. Except at the equator, where the globe was not stretched at all, the land masses were blown up in every direction. Greenland and the continents that reached towards the poles of the earth were stretched way out of shape. And as the lands were blown up, the distances between places in the polar region were stretched a great deal. Mercator knew that this was going to happen when he made his projection, but he was more interested in a chart that would show *direction* accurately than he was in the size and shape of continents. Somebody else could make a map or chart and project the globe in some other way if he wanted to show the true size and shape of things on earth.

Since the days of Gerard Mercator and Edward Wright a great many men have thought up ways of projecting or spreading out the globe on a sheet of paper. All of these projections are useful and all of them have their faults. When a sphere is stretched flat, something — either distance, direction, shape, or size — has to give. But no man has yet designed a better way of projecting the globe on straight lines for the use of navigators than Mercator. And for three hundred years the projection which was named after him has been used by sailors all over the world.

chapter *VII*

Beautiful Maps
to Sell

In the year 1440, or thereabouts, while Portuguese mariners under Henry the Navigator were driving their ships southward along the coast of Africa, a young German in the city of Strasbourg was putting the finishing touches on an invention that was going to prove far more valuable than black slaves or gold. His name was Johann Gutenberg. He was a secretive man and did not talk to many people. But like many another genius, he was poor, and he had to borrow money. And in order to borrow money, he had to tell somebody what he was up to and what he wanted the money for. So the word leaked out that this young man who came and went so silently was cutting separate letters of the alphabet in wood, and after arranging them into words and sentences, was "printing" a whole page of writing in a press, and doing it far quicker than any mortal scribe could do it by hand.

The people who made their living by copying with a pen the writings of others were not happy about the invention. It was a bad thing, they said, this printing of words on a machine. It would put men out of work. The scribes, the painters and goldsmiths who made a living copying and decorating manuscripts would starve. And if the wrong people got hold of the invention they could use the printing press to make thousands of copies of evil thoughts, and it might turn out to be an instrument of the devil himself.

In spite of the fuss people made about his invention, Gutenberg went ahead with his plans to "print" books in many copies so that a lot of people could read them. He also got the money he wanted to borrow. He worked very hard, and almost the first book he printed was the Holy Bible. It was a big book, and it took him a long time to set the type just the way he wanted it to look, but when he had finished the job and had printed it on the best paper he could find, it was beautiful. The letters were clear and spaced so that they were easy to read. Churches and monasteries bought copies and they were very happy to have them, because very few people could afford to have the whole Bible copied by hand. The printing press turned out to be such a useful and important invention that other men built presses and began to copy all kinds of books. It took a while for these printers to make money, because very few people knew how to read. Most of the readers in Europe were priests, doctors and lawyers, and a handful of scholars who sometimes traveled hundreds of miles just to look at a book. But by the year 1480 people were so thirsty for knowledge that printers were setting up shop in towns and cities all over Europe.

By the time Columbus discovered America, more than two hundred and thirty-eight towns in Europe and England had one or more printing presses, places where a book could be made and where printers impressed on their books the place where they were made and the date they were published. People became interested in reading, and before very long they were able to find a book in some place other than a church, a monastery or a school. So many people wanted to read that printers had to scurry around and find books they could print and sell to them. Their customers wanted to read something besides the Bible and schoolbooks, so the printers dug out some of the old manuscripts of the ancients and began to copy them.

In the libraries of churches and monasteries they found handwritten copies of books that were almost forgotten. They printed the pagan writings of the Greek and Latin philosophers, and the fables of Aesop. They found a copy of Strabo's *Geography* and they found a copy of Ptolemy's *Geographia*. These were the two most important discoveries of all for explorers and map makers, because they made them think about the whole wide world again: how big it was, and how it could be made into a picture, either on a globe or on a sheet of paper. Before Columbus had made his last voyage to America, more than seven printers had published the geographies of Strabo and Ptolemy. Many copies were sold.

Gutenberg's invention came along at just the right time, and the art of printing spread like wildfire across Europe. Every year, it seemed, there were more and more stories to be printed and published. Every year there was a little more to tell others. Knowledge could be traded back and forth in printed books. And after the New World was discovered and explorers brought back wonderful tales about the strange lands and strange people across the ocean, hundreds of books were printed to describe them. Many of these books were illustrated with pictures and maps.

In order to make these illustrations and maps, publishers depended on artists and goldsmiths who made a living by decorating all kinds of silver and gold objects with engraving.

The earliest known picture of a map maker at work was printed in 1598.

They did this by cutting very fine lines in the polished surface of the metal with delicate tools that had very sharp edges. The designs they cut were beautiful, and many artists and engravers wanted to keep a record of the work they had done. And this is the reason they finally taught themselves how to "print" pictures and maps to illustrate books.

Engraving on wood and metal was not a new idea, but Italian craftsmen showed the world how beautiful it could be. This is the way they did it. After cutting their design in the gold or silver they were decorating, they rubbed a gummy black ink into the cuts. Then they wiped the surface clean. After that they pressed a sheet of damp paper against the metal, and the ink that was stuck in the engraved lines came off on the paper in the form of a "print." This simple process made a nice clean copy of the design, and if the artist wanted to make more than one copy, all he had to do was rub more ink into the metal surface and print again.

After years of practice, artists began to engrave their designs and pictures on a sheet or plate of copper; first, because it was a cheaper metal than gold or silver, and second, because it could be hardened or tempered, and the engraved lines on the plate would not get fuzzy after a few prints had been made from it. This was very important after printers began to make as many as a thousand copies of a book. After the discovery of America there were more and more books and maps printed in editions of a thousand copies or more. Every year new books were written that told about the latest discoveries in the New World, and people were anxious to read them and look at the latest maps of America. Some of these new maps could be bought in separate sheets, but most of them were bound up in books and were used to illustrate the story the book had to tell.

In 1507, one of these maps, drawn and published by a man named Martin Waldseemüller came out with a new name on it. The name was "America," and on his map the name was spread

101

across the new lands that had been discovered by Columbus and explored by others after him. Waldseemüller called the New World "the fourth continent," and he explained to his readers that this land should be named after Amerigo Vespucci, because Vespucci had discovered it. Not many people agreed with him about the discovery, but his map was so popular and so many copies of it were printed that people got into the habit of calling the New World "America," and the name was accepted by everyone — even those who knew that Columbus had discovered it.

The business of printing and publishing books and maps was a great success. People everywhere wanted more and more books to read and look at. And because the Netherlands had trained some of the best engravers and printers in Europe, that was the place to go to find the best books and maps. By 1550 Antwerp had become the great commercial center of Western Europe. Her craftsmen were turning out thousands of prints of religious scenes, illustrating the lives of the saints, and stories from the Bible, all to be sold in the market place or exported to the Jesuit missions in South America.

The book-making industry in the Netherlands was well organized into guilds. Today we would call them unions. Some men made nothing but title pages and decorative borders for books. Others made nothing but ornaments for artists and architects. Still others made nothing but maps and charts. Their standards of workmanship were high. In their guilds or unions were "wardens" who supervised the work and saw to it that their men did not get careless. They were proud workmen.

Teerste Deel Veerde

Spieghel der Zeevaerdt, vande nauigatie der Westersche Zee, Innehoudende alle de Custe va Vranckryck Spaignen en t'principaelste deel van Engelandt, in diuersche Zee Caertē begrepē, met den gebruÿcke van dien, nu met grooter naerstichejt bÿ eē vergadert ē ghepractizeert, Door Lucas Iansz, Waghenaer. Piloot ofte Stuÿrman Residerende Inde vomaerde Zeesta dt Enchuÿsen.

Cum Priuilegio ad decennium.
Regni 5 8 3 Ma nis. et Cancellarie Brabantie

Ghedruct tot Leyden by Christoffel Plantyn
voor Lucas Jansz/ Waghenaer van Enckhuysen.
Anno M. D. LXXXV.

The title page of the first published sea atlas. Translated from the Dutch it reads *The Mariner's Mirrour*.

About this time two of the most important men in the history of map making were living and working in the Netherlands. One of them was Gerard Mercator, the man who made the first sensible chart for navigators. The other was Abraham Ortelius. Mercator had his shop in Duisburg, after moving from Louvain, and Ortelius worked in Antwerp, sixty miles away. They were competitors in the map business, but they were also friends, and each of them worked hard to improve the maps and charts that were being published all over Europe. They did it in different ways, because Mercator was a map *maker*, who went out with his men and remeasured the land that he wanted to map. Ortelius was a map *seller*, who began his career as a member of the guild that specialized in coloring maps and charts, the Guild of Saint Luke.

When Ortelius was a young man his father died, and the money he earned was not enough to support his mother and two sisters. In order to earn some more money he began to buy maps that were made in Antwerp and other places. His sisters mounted them on linen and Abraham colored them and sold them at the fairs in Frankfurt and other cities. Soon he began to travel abroad to find new markets for his Netherlands maps and to bring back maps that had been published in other countries. He visited France and Italy, where he sold his own beautifully colored maps and brought home copies of the best maps of foreign cities and countries he could find. In a few years he began to plan the first general atlas of the world, and this is how he happened to do it.

Ortelius had a good customer in Antwerp. His name was Hooftman, and he loved to collect and study maps. He was a

Abraham Ortelius of Antwerp (1527–1598) compiled and edited
the first general atlas of the world in modern times.

merchant, and he wanted to know as much about foreign countries and foreign markets as he could learn. But Hooftman grumbled about his maps. Some of them were big and bulky to handle. Some were so small that the print was hard to read. His eyes bothered him. What he wanted was a collection of maps, each one on a single sheet of paper, that he could read and study without getting a headache. He wanted good maps of the Netherlands, Germany, France and any other countries that could be bought. And he wanted them all the same size so that they could be bound up in a book and stored away on a shelf instead of being spread all over his office.

Abraham Ortelius was called in, and after he heard about Hooftman's problem he went home and began to gather up copies of all the maps he could find in his shop. He picked only the ones that were about the same size, and ended up with about thirty. He took them to a bookbinder and had them bound up in a handsome binding and then delivered the volume to his customer. Hooftman was so pleased with the job that Ortelius decided to make up a few more volumes of the same kind, and he was surprised to find that some of his other customers liked the idea, and the collection of maps as well.

Ortelius was happy about the maps he was selling, but he thought he could do even better if he searched a little harder for the very best maps of every country, and then published them himself in a book that was handsomely printed. He talked it over with Mercator, and his friend encouraged him to go ahead with the idea. He also talked with the best engravers he knew, and they told him they could make some of the large maps smaller so that they would fit the size Ortelius had picked for his book of maps.

It took Ortelius ten years to gather together the maps he wanted and have them engraved. When it came time to print the text for his atlas, Ortelius went to his good friend Christopher Plantin, one of the best printers in Europe, whose shop was in Antwerp. The two men decided to call the atlas *The Theater of the World,* and Plantin agreed to print it. There were thirty-five leaves of text and fifty-three maps in the book, and in May of 1570 it was published. The atlas sold so well that in three months a second edition was printed. So many foreigners wanted to buy it that Ortelius had the text translated, and when he died in 1598, at least twenty-eight editions of the big book had been published in Latin, Dutch, German, French, and Spanish.

During all the years Ortelius was selling his atlas, Mercator was working on the same kind of collection of maps, one that could be bound up in a single volume. But he had planned so many maps for his atlas that he did not live long enough to see it completed. However, the finished work was very popular, and copies of it sold for more than fifty years after it was first published. In order to make the atlas even more popular, and cheap enough for a poor man to buy, a pocket-size edition was published. The maps, of course, had to be re-engraved and reprinted, and many of them were very tiny and hard to read, but they were better than nothing to the people who wanted to know something about the world beyond their doorstep.

Geographical atlases became very popular books, and several publishers in Europe copied the ideas of Ortelius and Mercator.

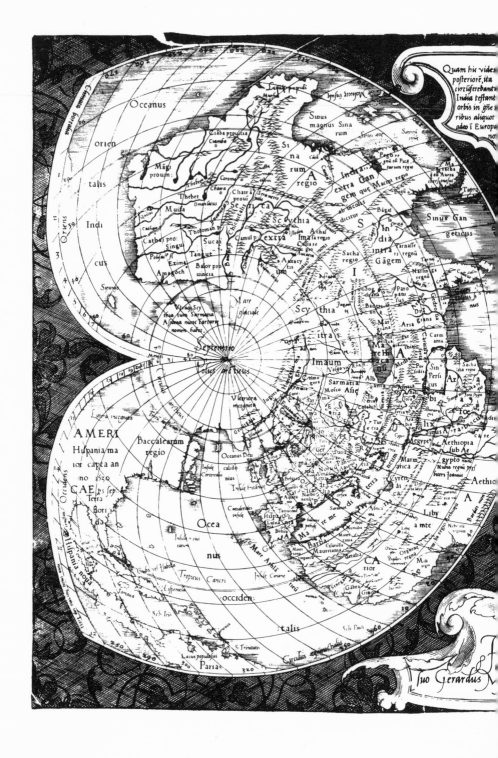

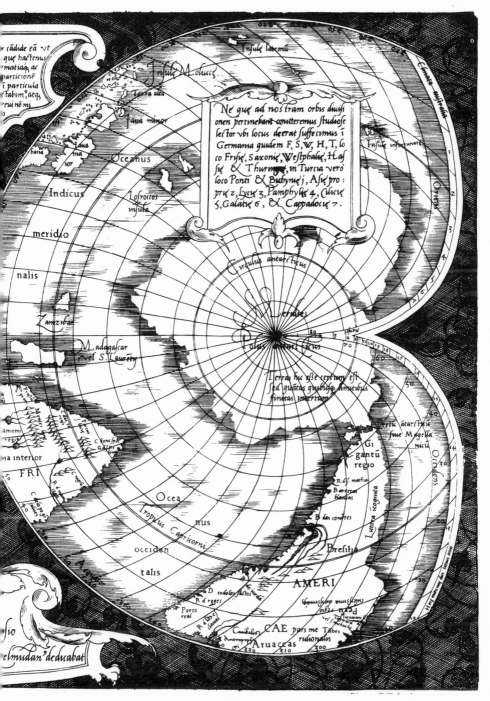

This map of the world, drawn more than four hundred years ago, was the first one to give a name to North America (*Americae ps. sep:*) and South America (*Americae pars meridionalis*).

One of these was an Italian named Lafreri. Lafreri is interesting to know about because of the title page of his atlas. Mercator had used the word *Atlas* in the title of his map collection instead of some other, such as *Theater of the World,* or *Looking Glass of the World.* Lafreri used the word *Atlas,* too, but he went a step further, and on the title page of his atlas he engraved the figure of the mighty Atlas of Greek mythology, supporting the world on his shoulders. He was the same hero that Homer had written about, and when he appeared on the title page of a book of maps, both his name and his picture, the public liked it, because he represented what the book was trying to tell its readers about — the world. Map publishers tried many other names for their geographic volumes, but the word *atlas* pleased their readers best, and today it is used by geographers all over the world. Everyone knows what it means, and what they can expect to find in the book — a collection of maps.

Nearly a hundred years after Ortelius was born, one of the most famous map makers of Europe published his first atlas. His name was Willem Janszoon Blaeu, and he had his printing house in Amsterdam. Blaeu was a scholar and scientist as well as a printer and publisher of maps. One of his visitors described the shop where Blaeu and his two sons made books and atlases. The building stood near the canal in Amsterdam. It was a hundred and fifty feet long and seventy-five feet wide.

> Fronting on the canal is a room with cases in which the copper plates are kept, from which the Atlases, the Books of the Cities of the Netherlands and foreign countries, also the Mariners' Atlas and other choice books are printed, and

Gerard Mercator (1512–1594) did much to change the art of map making to an exact science.

which must have cost a ton of gold. Next to this is a press-room used for plate printing, and opening upon the cross street is a place where the type, from which impressions have been made, is washed. Then follows in order the room for book printing, which resembles a long hall with many windows on both sides. In the extreme rear is a room in which the type and certain other materials are stored. Opposite this storeroom is a stairway leading to a small room above which is set apart for the use of the proof-readers, where first and second impressions are carefully looked over and the errors corrected which have been made by the type-setters. In front of this last room is a long table or bench on which the final prints are placed as soon as they are brought from the press, and where they are left for a con-siderable time. Over the room occupied by the proof-readers is the type foundry where the letters used in the printing of the various languages are molded.

There were other remarkable things about the Blaeu print-ing office that their visitor did not mention. There were nine big flat-bed presses that were used for the printing of books, and six more that were used for printing maps and pictures from engraved copper plates. With this fine equipment the Blaeus were able to print the biggest book that any customer would want. They could also print it well, because the people who worked for the Blaeus were the best pressmen, engravers and color artists in the Netherlands.

The most famous book printed and published by the Blaeu firm was their *Atlas Major,* a mammoth atlas in twelve volumes. Very few printing houses in Europe could have afforded to make it, because of the expense involved and the number of

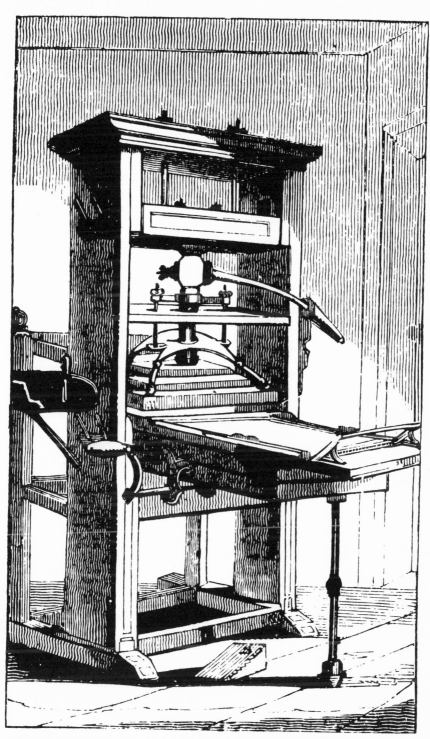

This printing press was designed by Willem Janszoon Blaeu, map maker and publisher. It was copied and used by printers for nearly two hundred years.

copper plates that were used to engrave the maps, and the thousands of pieces of type that were needed to print the text. It took almost thirty years to draw and engrave the six hundred maps that filled it. Then it took still more time for the artists to color and decorate the maps and the big initial letters in the text. The bindings were made of a white polished leather called vellum, and they were decorated with ornamental designs filled with pure gold leaf instead of color.

The Blaeu atlas never was and never will be a poor man's book, but many geographers think that it is the most beautiful collection of maps that has ever been made. At the time it was first published, in 1663, a copy was specially bound in royal purple and presented to the Sultan Mohammed IV. He was so pleased with its beauty and the number of valuable maps it contained that he ordered his geographers to translate the whole thing, including the place names on the maps, into the Turkish language.

At the time the Blaeus and other map publishers were turning out their wares, there were many different ways of showing mountains, rivers, roads, mines and forests on a map. Each country had its own signs and symbols for these things. But after years of exchanging maps and charts back and forth between different countries, map makers began to realize that it would be helpful to everyone if all these symbols for roads and mountains, anchorages and so on, were made the same way on all maps and charts, and some of them tried to co-operate. On the better maps cities and towns were usually shown by dots, small circles, or by a miniature picture of a castle or a fort with flying pennants. Coastlines were shaded with fine lines (hachures) to make them stand out. Anchorages for ships were marked with a tiny anchor, and shoal water was indicated by tiny dots (stippling).

Some map publishers used different colors instead of other symbols to tell their readers the various things their maps would show. And some of the materials they used to color their maps were strange. The hen's egg was one of the most popular. The egg white was a favorite "size" to make the color stick to the paper, and it could be used as a glaze instead of shellac or varnish. One map artist wrote that if egg white was strained through a clean linen cloth and an equal amount of the best white vinegar was added to it, it would keep for a long time.

The yolk of the egg was used for another purpose. If one wanted to make white letters on a black background, the yolk was first ground up or beaten, and a little water added. The lettering was done with this mixture, either with a brush or pen. Then the whole sheet of paper or parchment was covered with black ink. After the ink was dry the paper was rubbed with a clean cloth, and the part that had been covered with the egg yolk would rub clean and be perfectly white.

There were two kinds of black that artists liked to use for coloring maps. One of them was sable or fume black, which was nothing more than lamp black. To collect it for painting, a torch or candle was held under a metal pan or basin and allowed to smoke the bottom. Then the black was scraped off and mixed with a little white of egg. The other black was like velvet, and it was made by burning the antler of a stag or deer in a hot furnace until it was a black powder. Then white of egg was added and mixed thoroughly. The two blacks

115

were quite different, and both of them were beautiful colors.

In order to make colored maps even more beautiful, artists used to lay gold leaf over some of their colors. First they drew the design they wanted to decorate with a fine brush dipped in garlic juice. Then they laid the gold leaf on the map with a very soft rabbit's foot or camel's-hair brush. After being allowed to dry for a day or more the whole surface was rubbed with a soft cloth, and the parts that had been painted with the garlic juice held the gold leaf and the rest wiped off.

Artists thought up many other ways of making maps beautiful, and most of their colors have stayed fresh and bright after hundreds of years of wear, weather and light. But artists warned people that if the paper on which the map was engraved was not strong and clean, the colors would sink in and smear in the wrong places. They said also that there was more than one way to color a map, but that some ways were better than others. For example, seashores and lakes should be colored a light indigo. The borders of the map should be colored either yellow or crimson to make them stand out. Then if there were such things as forests shown on the map, each tree should be dabbed with grass green. Towns and cities should be colored with red lead or some other color that would make them stand out. Political boundaries between countries should be colored copper green.

The old wind-blowers of ancient times were not forgotten in the drawing and coloring of maps. Eurus, the east wind, was supposed to be shown as a young boy with cheeks puffed out and with a gentle breeze blowing from his mouth. He should have wings on his shoulders. Zephyrus, the west wind, should be drawn as a young person with a merry look on his face, as though he were about to sing. Boreas, the north wind, should be drawn like an old grouch, with a terrible look on his face, and with snow or icicles on his beard. Auster, the south wind, was a disagreeable fellow, and he should be drawn "with head and wings wet, and with a pot or urn pouring forth water, with which descend frogs, grasshoppers, and other creatures that are bred by moisture."

Between the years 1650 and 1700, there were eighteen map-making centers in Europe. The art of line engraving and picture making was taught in all these places, and it was taught well. The technique of reproducing maps that were well drawn and beautifully colored was so good that there were almost no improvements made in it until the invention of the lithographic process of printing, more than a hundred years later. What map publishers needed in 1650 were good maps to copy and publish, and at that time there were very few of them to be had.

Nearly all of Europe and parts of Asia and Africa had been surveyed after a fashion, but even the best of the maps of these continents were none too good. Instead of checking distances and directions between different places, lazy map makers copied the maps of others and published them with all their mistakes. And every year there were so many new discoveries being made in the New World that it was impossible for map makers to keep up with them. Besides, it was cheaper to just keep printing an old map than to have artists and engravers make a lot of expensive changes on an old map plate or engrave a new one.

In 1650 the map of the habitable world needed enlarging

in all directions, but just how much it had grown, no man knew. Where did new places belong in relation to other places? Who had checked the distances and directions across the Western Sea? European monarchs had staked out claims in foreign lands, including the New World, yet not one of them could locate the territory he claimed. For this reason map makers were forced to turn again to science before further progress could be made, and science was ready with many of the answers.

chapter VIII

The Science
of Latitude

During all the years that map makers were learning new ways to make maps beautiful so that people would want to buy them, scientists of all kinds were helping them to make their maps more accurate. They were trying to find better ways of finding the latitude and longitude of places so that a person could go to a map or globe and spot what he was looking for without any trouble. It was not an easy job. They invented a great many instruments that were designed to measure the height of the sun from the horizon or the height of the North Star. They knew a great deal about the sun and how it behaved. They also knew that the North Star stayed in its proper place in the heavens while the other stars revolved around it. The ancients knew what should be done to measure the angles that would tell them the latitude of a place, but they did not have the instruments that were invented hundreds of years later.

The astrolabe, or star measurer, that Ptolemy wrote about was a good instrument for measuring angles, and most of the great explorers, including Christopher Columbus, used one to find the latitude. But this was not easy to use aboard a ship that was tossing and pitching in a rough sea. Mariners tried to

119

use it just the same, and whenever they were lost they tried to go ashore and set up their astrolabe on the beach so that they could find out how far above or below the equator they were.

The astrolabe was a very simple instrument, as Ptolemy described it, but it could be made to do all kinds of measuring. As time went on men learned how to improve it. They made it more accurate by fitting glass lenses to both ends of the swinging vane so that whatever a person was sighting at would look sharper and the measurements would be more accurate. Astrolabes were made large and small. Some of them were pocket-size and some were several feet in diameter. The biggest were made of iron or brass, trussed and braced so that they would not warp and become inaccurate. Most of the big ones were built for astronomers, and they were set up in observatories where the stars and other heavenly bodies could be studied and mapped.

Astrolabes that were made for mariners were heavy and were from five to seven inches across. The weight of the instrument kept it from swinging around in the wind when a man was trying to take a sight of the sun or a star. They often had a plumb line attached to the top with a weight or bob at the end, so that the man who was taking the sight would know when the instrument was hanging vertically and the ninety-degree mark on the circle was pointed at the horizon. One inventor thought he had a good idea when he designed a chair that could be swung between the masts of a ship so that the navigator who was trying to measure the height of the sun would not be troubled by the rolling ocean. It was not a very good idea, and it was probably never used.

The cross-staff was another instrument used by ancient astronomers to find the latitude of places and the angle between two stars. In many ways it was as good an instrument as the astrolabe. Besides, it was easy to handle and cheaper to make. Geographers and mariners used it as far back as the Crusades. It had different names in different languages. Some called it a "Jacob's staff"; some called it a "sighting stick." The Spanish and Portuguese sailors called it the "staff of Saint James" (the patron saint of pilgrims and travelers) because of its shape. The French thought it looked very much like a crossbow, and they called it the *arbalète*. The English called it the "cross-staff." It was used all over Europe, and no one knows who invented it.

There were five parts to the cross-staff, the cross and three sights. The staff or "yard" was simply a stick of wood about 1¼ inches square and about 36 inches long. The cross, or transom, was usually about 1¾ inches thick and 2½ inches wide. The crosspiece was pierced in the center by a square hole or mortise cut so that it would fit snugly on the staff but loose enough to slide freely back and forth along it. The crosspiece had two peephole sights, one at either end, and there was a third peephole on the near end of the long staff. In order to measure the angle between the horizon and the sun, the trick was to line up the three sights so that the upper one on the cross was pointed directly at the sun and the lower one was pointed at the horizon.

All you had to do then was slide the cross backward or forward along the staff until the three sights were lined up and you had the three angles of a triangle. On the early cross-staff

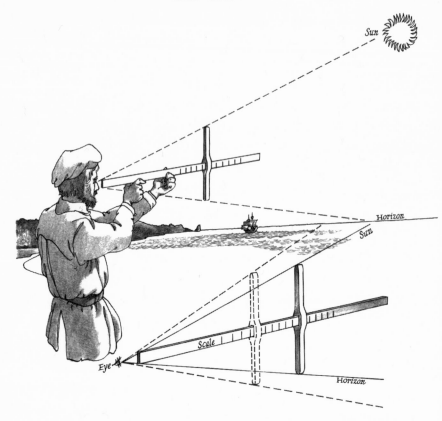

The cross-staff, or Jacob's staff, a crude instrument, was used for centuries to measure the height of the sun. Its chief fault lay in the fact that the sun's rays were blinding to the observer.

there were no marks or graduations to tell a man how much of an angle he had measured, and he had to lay the instrument on a table and do some figuring. On the later cross-staffs, the top side of the staff was measured off into degrees and minutes of arc so that angles could be read off in no time at all.

The astrolabe and cross-staff were good instruments, and

122

The back-staff was an invention of John Davis of Sandridge, who described it in a book entitled *The Seaman's Secrets*, published in 1607.

they helped many a map maker and navigator to find his latitude, but there was one thing wrong with them. The man who was taking a sight with either instrument had to look directly into the sun. Even when the peepholes were fitted with smoked glass, as some of them were, there was enough glare on a bright day to blind him a little, and the angles he measured were not as accurate as they should be. It took a long time for somebody to think of a way to measure the height of the sun without looking directly at it. But finally an English mariner named John Davis thought of a way to make a cross-staff so that a person would not have to look into the sun's eye at all.

Davis called his instrument the back-staff, because the person using it worked with his back to the sun. He described it in a little book called *The Seaman's Secrets* that was published in the year 1607. The first back-staff he designed was as simple as the cross-staff. It had a long staff graduated into degrees and minutes of arc so that it could be read without laying it on a table. It also had a transom that slid back and forth on the staff, but instead of being a regular crosspiece, it was a half-cross, with the lower part cut off. There was an eyepiece for the observer to peep through and a narrow slit at the far end of the staff.

In order to take a sight and measure the height of the sun, the observer held the back-staff up and aimed the two sights on the long staff so that he could see the horizon through the slit at the far end. Then, with his right hand, he moved the transom down along the staff until it cast a shadow that fell on the staff right at the slit at the far end of the staff. Then he could read off his angle from the top of the staff.

Several other inventors besides John Davis worked to improve the back-staff and make it more accurate. Some of them were navigators like Davis, and some were astronomers. Edward Wright, the mathematician and chart-maker, was one of them. Edmund Halley, the astronomer, was much interested in the instrument. French scientists studied ways of improving it.

One hundred years after John Davis first described the simple back-staff, very little remained of it except the reflecting principle — working with the sun behind one, and lining up the horizon and either the shadow cast by the sun or the reflection of the sun itself. Instead of using a graduated staff to mark off the angle of the sun, inventors came up with a better idea. The instruments they made were called quadrants when they were shaped like a quarter of a circle, octants when they were one eighth of a circle, and sextants when they were a sixth part of a circle.

Some of these instruments were big and awkward to handle. Some of them had more gadgets on them than were really necessary. But every year some inventor made little improvements in the instrument that made it easier to handle and more accurate as a measuring device. Some of them were fitted with small telescopes so that the sight at the horizon would be sharper. Some were graduated into very fine divisions of a circle so that navigators could read off the height of the sun in minutes of arc as well as degrees.

Modern sextants that sea captains and airplane navigators use are very much the same as the instruments that were made two hundred years ago. The difference is that they are more accurate. But they use the same ideas. With a system of mirrors and small pieces of smoked glass they spot the sun, and instead of lining up the horizon with the shadow cast by the sun, they bring the image of the sun itself right down so that it seems to be sitting on the horizon when a person takes a sight. One of the handiest improvements that has been made in the instrument in the past few years is a built-in bubble, the same kind of a bubble that carpenters have built into their levels. The bubble sextant allows a navigator to measure the height of a star when there is no horizon to peer at. Airplane navigators use it when they could not possibly use any other kind of sextant. The bubble sextant today is so efficient that it seems impossible that any inventor could improve it, but who knows what some young men will think up tomorrow that will make the instrument even better?

It was a fine thing to have an instrument for navigators and map makers that would accurately measure the height of the sun, the moon or any of the other heavenly bodies. But there

The navigator on this early ship sits in a swinging chair to find the height of a star and his latitude. The invention was never used.

was still a big problem left to solve. All scientists knew about it. In fact the ancient astronomers knew about it. They knew after watching the heavenly bodies for thousands and thousands of years that except for Polaris, the North Star, every star in the heavens rose and set in a different position each night, just as the sun rises and sets at a different height each day. This meant that if a person measured the angle of the sun on Tuesday, January 23, of any one year, it would be a little bit different the next day at high noon. That meant that the latitude he was trying to measure would change each day.

The early astronomers may not have understood exactly why these things were so, but they knew that they happened. They may not have known that the earth revolves around the sun and that its axis is tilted at an angle. And they may not have known that as the earth spins on its axis around the sun it has a little wobble to it like a football that is spinning through the air. But they did know about the changes they saw in the position of the sun by day and the stars by night. For this reason they made calendars and timetables for each of the heavenly bodies, so that when they measured the latitude of a place, either from the height of the sun or the height of a star, they could correct it with their timetables and their calendars.

These facts about the heavenly bodies were all set down on paper, and after the invention of printing they were published in the form of a book that we call an "almanac." The early almanacs were put together by astronomers and mathematicians who knew about such things. The timetables of the sun were figured out with the calendar of days that everybody used. If a navigator measured the height of the sun from the horizon at noon on a certain day of the year, he could go to his almanac and see what the timetable for the sun was for that day, and with the help of a little arithmetic he would be able to figure out his *true* latitude instead of the latitude his sextant told him it was.

The sextant and *Nautical Almanac* are still two of the best friends of navigators and map makers, but what if the sun does not shine during the day? Then one must wait for the night and hope it will be clear enough to see the stars, or at least the polestar and the Little Bear. People knew and wrote about the Little Bear at least three thousand years ago. They knew that he swings around the top of the heavens each night, the end of his tail pinned to the North Star. And they knew that the North Star was not exactly at the top of the heavens. It was a little bit to one side, so that each night it swung around the top of the heavens in a very small circle.

Like the changes in the position of the sun each day, astronomers figured out how big a circle the North Star described each twenty-four hours and how far above the celestial pole or how far below it the star would be at a certain hour of the night. Each night the position of the Little Bear or Little Dipper was a little bit different. The Bear was tilted one way or another, because when the sandglass or some other kind of timekeeper said it was midnight "by the clock," the stars were keeping their own time, which is almost four minutes slower than the day we have divided into twenty-four hours for the sake of convenience.

More than seven hundred years ago a man thought up a

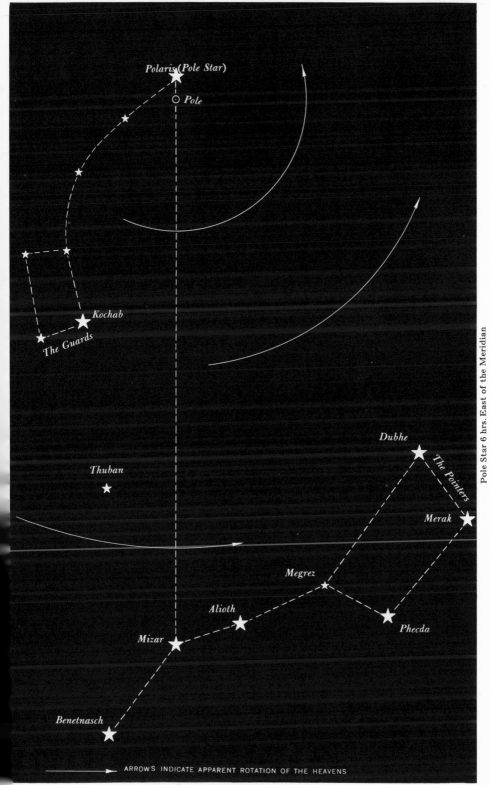

The two Bears (the Big Dipper and Little Dipper) have been used for hundreds of years to tell the hour of the night and the latitude of different places.

way of making the Little Bear tell people the time of night and the latitude of a place above the equator on any day of the year. He was Raymond Lully, and he wrote about his invention in about the year 1290. He called his instrument a "nocturnal," and it was a very clever one. It was a wooden wheel with a handle on it and a peephole in the middle. The wheel had three disks of different sizes inside the frame, that swung around in a circle. The outer circle was divided into the days and months of the year. The next smaller disk was divided into the hours and minutes of the day and night. The innermost circle was devoted to the figure of a little man named Kochab, who was named after a star in the Little Dipper, or Little Bear. Kochab is the brightest star in the Little Dipper, and is one of the "Guards" along the outer edge of the dipper, opposite the handle, that are in the same position as the "pointers" on the Big Dipper. Kochab swung around the inner circle with his arms outstretched and with a hole in his midriff, which was the peephole to sight through. His head, feet and two outstretched arms marked off the four quarters of the circle. But his inventor, instead of naming these divisions of the circle the way the points of the compass are named, labeled them Head, Foot, East Arm and West Arm. The four intermediate points, or divisions of Kochab, were called East Shoulder, West Shoulder, Line below East Arm, Line below West Arm. Why the inventor of the nocturnal picked on little Kochab, no one will ever know.

In one operation a navigator could make the necessary correction in the height of the polestar by using the nocturnal. After getting the height of the star with a quadrant or sextant he held up the nocturnal and peeped through Kochab's middle. First he turned the fellow so that his head pointed at the star Kochab. The calendar disk was turned to the right position and the hour disk was also adjusted, and then the correction could be read off from the instrument. The polestar was either at a level with the celestial pole or it was above or below it

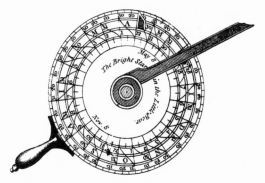

A nocturnal built two hundred years ago. By peeking through the hole in the center and adjusting the movable disks around it, the observer could tell the hour of the night and the latitude of his position.

on one side or the other. The correction that was made with the nocturnal was important, because four hundred years ago the difference in the latitude could amount to fifty miles or more, and that was enough to get a ship into serious trouble.

Today navigators do not have to depend on the nocturnal to make corrections in the height of the polestar. In the *American Nautical Almanac,* the navigator's bible that he would not be without, there are four "tables" that tell all about Polaris and what position the star will be in at a certain time of night and on a given day of the year.

The sun, moon and stars change position in the sky each day. Not very much, but enough to make a difference to the people who are trying to make accurate measurements of latitude. For this reason astronomers and mathematicians spend millions of hours peering through their telescopes and plotting with charts and mathematical tables just where in the sky a certain star or the sun will be on any day or night of the year. And in spite of wars, scientists all over the world exchange this information, and many countries publish almanacs that anyone can buy and anyone can read.

chapter IX

The Science
of Longitude

The measurement of longitude was the most difficult problem early map makers had to face, and it was the last one to be solved. It happened in France during the reign of Louis XIV, who was born in 1638 and died in 1715. Centuries before, the ancients knew perfectly well the tools that were needed to make accurate maps: an accurate way of measuring both the latitude and longitude of a place — any place on the face of the earth. But they did not have the instruments to do it with.

French scientists who worked for Louis XIV had two instruments that the ancients did not have: a telescope and a good timekeeper. These two instruments made all the difference in the world. With them map makers were able to make the first really accurate maps and charts, and for the first time in history it was possible to find the longitude of any place, either on land or at sea.

Every map maker who worked in the field measuring land, and every navigator who sailed the seas, was anxiously waiting for someone to invent a scheme for measuring longitude, "the east-west line" as it was called. How to do it was the big question. Some of the men who studied the problem got very discouraged and gave it up as a bad job. Others decided that it was such a hopeless problem to solve that it was not worth bothering about. A man named Pigafetta, who sailed with Magellan, wrote that when a pilot or navigator of his time was able to find his latitude at sea he felt lucky and quite proud of himself. In fact, he felt so lucky and so proud that he decided to let someone else worry about the longitude. These men did not even try. They did not have the education, and they thought they did not have the time.

In spite of the fact that many people were lazy and many did not care, the time came when something had to be done. The habitable world had expanded, and trade routes that Strabo and Ptolemy never dreamed of were spread out across the globe. As the years rolled by, it became more and more important to have accurate maps and charts and to have a way of measuring the number of degrees of longitude between places and the number of miles.

The real trouble began in the year 1493, less than two months after Christopher Columbus returned to Spain with the news of a great discovery. Portugal was not happy about what he said he had found, and claimed that Spain had no right to the new lands. Spain thought differently. There was trouble brewing, and in order to prevent a war between the two strongest maritime nations in the world, Pope Alexander VI stepped in to settle the argument. He unrolled a big chart of the world, and on it he drew a meridian line, north and south, from pole to pole, out in the Western Ocean *one hundred leagues west of the Azore Islands.* Then he said that Spain should have all the lands not already belonging to any other

134

Christian prince or king, which had been discovered, or that might be discovered west of that line. And he granted to Portugal all the lands that had been discovered or might be discovered to the east of the line. This decision, which was carefully written down, was called the Bull of Demarcation.

It was a very nice way to settle an argument and prevent a war, except for the fact that no one, including the Pope, had the slightest idea where a line drawn on the map *one hundred leagues west of the Azores* could be found on the face of the earth or the surface of the ocean. There was no way of measuring the distance out in the ocean; in fact, there was no way of measuring *any* great distance across the earth from east to west. Meanwhile armed convoys from Spain and Portugal plowed back and forth across the Atlantic Ocean, and their captains never knew when or where they would sight dry land. Sometimes they reached an island or a strange coast much sooner than they expected they would, and their ships went on the rocks and were lost. All such losses were costly, both in lives and precious cargo.

Every loaded ship that came home safely from faraway places, whether it was from the Spice Islands of the Indies or the New World, was worth a fortune, and neither Spain nor Portugal could afford to lose one and let the other country get ahead in the world of trade. It was a serious business, and the key to the control of world trade was some kind of scheme for finding a ship's position at sea, both its latitude and its longitude.

Things went from bad to worse, and in 1598, King Philip III of Spain decided that he was going to do something about

135

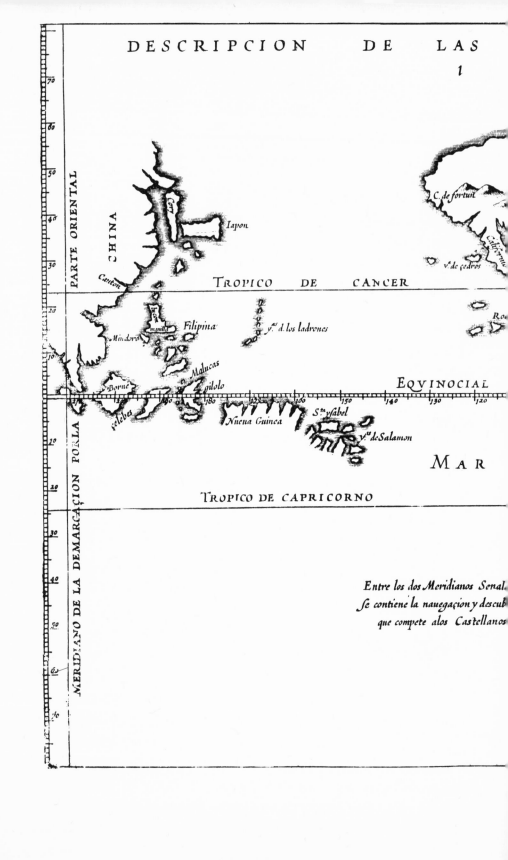

PARTE ORIENTAL

MERIDIANO DE LA DEMARCAÇION PORLA

CHINA

Corz

Iapon

C. de fortun

California

v.ª de çedros

Canton

TROPICO   DE   CANCER

Leon

maniIa

Filipina

y.ªˢ d. los ladrones

R. o

Mindoro

Malucas

gilolo

Borne

EQVINOCIAL

celebes

170 160 0 180 170 160 150 140 130 120

Nueua Guinea

Sta yſabel

y.ᵘ deSalamon

MAR

TROPICO DE CAPRICORNO

Entre los dos Meridianos Senal
ſe contiene la nauegaçion y descu
que compete alos Castellanos

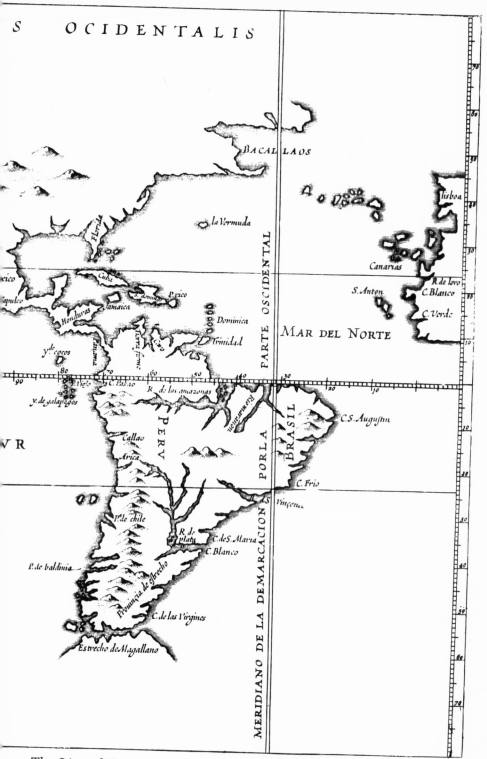

The Line of Demarcation laid down by Pope Alexander VI gave Spain full right to all discoveries west of the Line to the halfway mark around the world. Portugal was granted full control over all new discoveries east of the Line to the halfway mark.

the problem of measuring the longitude at sea. First he called his scientists and sea captains together and asked them for advice. They had no ideas to offer. So King Philip posted a reward, offering a lifetime pension of six thousand ducats and a bonus of a thousand more to anyone who could solve the problem of measuring the longitude. Not only that, he offered smaller prizes to anyone who just had a good idea, one that scientists could use to develop a system of finding the longitude.

Other countries decided to do the same thing, and in a very short time not only Spain, but Portugal, Venice and Holland had posted rewards. Then there was a wild scramble to see who would win the prizes. Many people, including crazy inventors, had ideas, but nearly all of them were impractical. King Philip got bored and disgusted by the men who flocked to his court to tell him that they had found the *real* answer to the problem. He got so bored, in fact, that when an Italian scientist named Galileo wrote him a letter in 1616, telling him that he thought he had an answer to the problem, the king paid no attention. That time he was wrong. Galileo tried hard to convince the Spanish court that he had a good idea, and some of the scientists in Spain must have been half convinced, because they corresponded with him off and on for sixteen years. After that Galileo got tired of writing letters.

Holland was more polite to Galileo, and when he finally wrote to the Dutch government and told them his scheme for measuring longitude, they were interested instead of bored, and they treated him like a gentleman and a scholar. He was able to correspond with a committee of scientific experts who were appointed to be the judges of any ideas and inventions for finding the longitude. One of those experts was Willem Blaeu, the map maker and map publisher. Letters went back and forth between Italy and Holland. The scientists of Holland and the States General, their governing body, were much impressed. They approved of Galileo and his idea, and as a mark of respect and admiration for all he had done for science, they presented him with a gold chain, and they hoped that one of their experts could visit him in Italy some day and find out more about his scheme. For several reasons the trip was never made, and Holland was the loser. But Galileo was not forgotten by the world, and his idea did not die.

Galileo found in the heavens the answer to the problem of measuring the longitude. He was a stargazer. Several years before he wrote his first letter to the court of Spain he had built an instrument called a telescope. It was a simple machine, nothing more than a metal tube with magnifying lenses at both ends. But it was a wonderful machine because it made it possible for mankind to see stars in the heavens that had never been seen before. Galileo not only gazed at the stars with his telescope, he studied them carefully and timed them with his clock. After studying them on every clear night for many years, he decided that he had found a first-rate timekeeper in the sky. It was the planet Jupiter and its satellites, the four small stars that he was able to see revolving around its equator. The satellites were stars that could not be seen with the naked eye. Around and around they went across the face of Jupiter, first on one side of the planet and then on the other, first appearing and then disappearing on the other side. At least two of them disappeared (were eclipsed) every two days, so

Galileo Galilei (1564–1642) discovered Jupiter's satellites.

that a person watching them did not have to wait and watch too long for the hands of their celestial clock to move around.

Now how could any timekeeper be the answer to the problem of measuring longitude? The answer is quite simple. The

J. D. Cassini (1625–1712) used them to determine longitude.
The Paris Observatory is in the background.

earth had been divided by ancient geographers into 360 degrees
of longitude. It had also been divided into twenty-four hours
of clock time. These hours represented one full day, or one

complete rotation of the earth on its axis. These things being so, it did not take a genius to figure out that in one hour by the clock the earth had spun around through 15 degrees of longitude, or that every four minutes by the clock the earth had rotated one degree of longitude on its axis.

Galileo said his scheme would work if only two things were known: (1) the circumference of the earth and (2) the difference in local clock time between two different places at once.

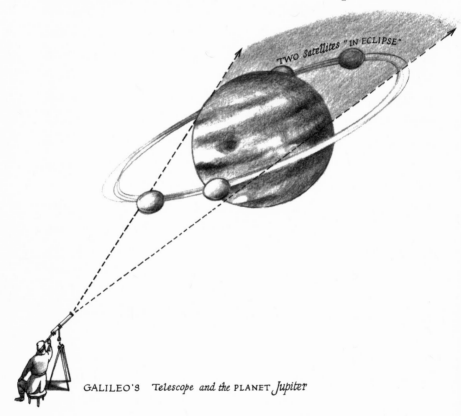

GALILEO'S *Telescope and the* PLANET *Jupiter*

The planet Jupiter (greatly enlarged) with four of its satellites, which served as a celestial timekeeper for many years.

Scientists thought they had come pretty close to measuring the circumference of the earth and the length of a degree, but no one had figured out a way to compare local clock time in two places at the very same moment. In order to compare the two and figure out the difference, there would have to be some kind of a signal between the two places, so that a person in Paris and another one in Jamaica would be looking at their clocks and telling the time at the very same second. Today signals can be sent from one place to another by telegraph, by telephone and by radio, but it was not so when Galileo was alive. Today any person can hear the beep-beep of the time signals that are broadcast all over the world, but Galileo had to depend on the planet Jupiter and its satellites, his celestial clock, to send out a signal that could be seen if not heard around the world by anyone with a telescope.

Two kinds of time are kept in the world. One of these is star time, the time it takes for the heavens to make one complete round trip across the sky. This kind of time is about four minutes slower than the kind of time our clocks keep, because the stars pay no attention to people or the sun. It is the standard time used by astronomers, and the stars are dependable. The other kind of time is *local* or *mean* time. This is the kind of time the clock on the wall and the radio announcer say it is. Local time is sun time, and at high noon in any city or village in the world, the sun is directly south, and it has climbed as high as it is going for that particular day. It will be back tomorrow, headed directly south at high noon, even though it will be a little higher or a little lower in the sky, depending on the season of the year. Local time or sun time is just a convenient way of dividing up the twenty-four-hour day so that people around the world will know when to get up, when to go to bed, when to feed the chickens and when to milk the cows.

Today astronomers and navigators can tune in on the radio or pick up the telephone and find out the local time in any part of the world and figure out for themselves the difference in hours and minutes, or the difference in longitude. And if Galileo had used the phone he might have said, "This is Galileo talking. My clock says it is midnight over here, and exactly three seconds ago the third satellite of Jupiter disappeared behind the face of the planet. I hope you were watching it as well as your clock, and I hope you set down the exact hour, minute and second that it disappeared. If you did, what did your clock read? If you can tell me, we can figure out how far we are apart." Today this imaginary conversation is not imaginary. It takes place every hour of the day, only instead of conversation over the phone, we hear little beeps on the radio that tell the same story.

Galileo had a first-rate idea for measuring the longitude. He also furnished the key to the construction of a very accurate timekeeper. The careful experiments he had made for years with the simple pendulum, which was nothing but a weight that swung from the end of a string, were the answers to the problem.

The ancients told the time of day and night by using sundials, sandglasses, and even water clocks that dripped the hours and minutes away, drop by drop, the same way the sandglass or hourglass told the time as the sand trickled through a tiny hole in a glass tube. But none of these time-keepers was accurate enough for astronomers or other scientists. They were looking for some kind of a timekeeper that could be driven by controlled power and precision-adjusted without much trouble. One or two people had tried to make a clock of cogs and wheels with weights attached, but these machines were not very successful. However, in 1657 a Dutch astronomer named Christian Huygens built a clock, the grandfather of all the fine timekeepers which have been used by scientists ever since. He put together all the cogs and wheels and weights that other men had tried to use and made them work.

After he had studied Galileo's experiments with the simple pendulum, Huygens decided that a swinging weight might be a good way of controlling the speed of the wheels and cogs of a clock as the weights pulled them around and around. Instead of coming down with a bang, with wheels flying and hands spinning, the weights would come down slowly, one notch at a time, one notch every time the pendulum swung this way or that.

The beautiful thing about the pendulum clock that Huygens built was that it could be regulated to keep very accurate time, and after it had been used for a number of years people began to call pendulum clocks "regulators." They were what we call "grandfather" clocks. Galileo had discovered that the longer the pendulum the longer it took the swinging weight or "bob" at the end of it to make one trip back and forth. Huygens studied it even more carefully, and found that, sure enough, the length of time it took for a swinging pendulum

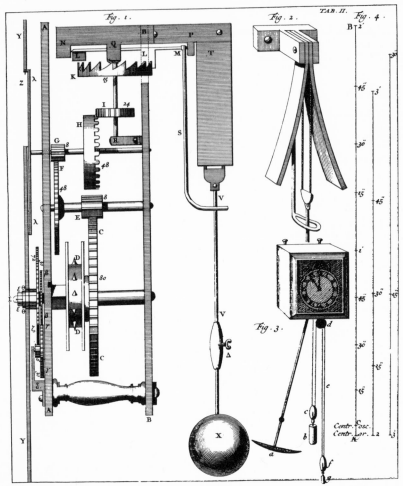

The clock built by Christian Huygens was the grandfather of all accurate timekeepers. This simple diagram shows how it worked.

to make one round trip could be figured out mathematically. He attached an adjustment screw just below the bob. By turning the screw one way or the other he could shorten the pendulum and make his clock run faster, or he could lengthen it and make it run slower. He also figured out exactly how long a pendulum would have to be to make a clock beat out one second exactly, every time it swung from one side to the other. For three hundred years since then, pendulum clocks have been ticking away the hours, minutes and seconds, and until very recently they were the favorite timekeepers of astronomers and other scientists.

The invention of the pendulum clock came at the very time the more powerful nations of Europe were in the middle of the race to see which of them would be the first to solve the riddle of the longitude. Every year more and more people were beginning to realize how important a race it was, and every year the prizes were getting fatter. In the seventeenth century the project was every bit as important to the world as the atom bombs and space missiles are today. Sailors and navigators were not the only ones concerned about the problem. European monarchs were fighting over lands that they knew very little about. Most of them did not even know where the boundaries of their own countries were located. They talked about them and they fought over them, but their maps were precious little help when it came to locating them and settling boundary disputes.

One of the European monarchs most interested in having better maps of his own country was Louis XIV of France, who was mixed up in all kinds of wars with his neighbors. Like King Philip of Spain, Louis XIV took his problem to the experts, and fortunately one of the best of them was his principal minister, Jean Colbert, a clever man and a fine scholar.

Colbert convinced his king that the way to get better maps and charts of the world and of France was to organize a scientific academy and bring together the best experts that could be found, no matter where they lived. He was sure that if such a group could be organized many problems could be solved, including the measurement of longitude and the improvement of maps and charts. Louis XIV listened and agreed to try the experiment.

In 1666 the Royal Academy of Sciences was founded, and Jean Colbert invited the best scientists in Europe to come and work in France. Among them was Christian Huygens, who brought along his pendulum clock. These men were offered handsome salaries and a comfortable place to live. Most of those who were invited to Paris accepted the invitation, and in a short time the Academy was filled with people who knew how to do all kinds of things. Some of them were astronomers, some were mathematicians. There were even a few physicians and biologists. All of them were expert mechanics and knew how to make telescopes, how to grind lenses, and how to make any of the instruments that astronomers and map makers might want to use. Many of them were inventors.

These remarkable men convinced the king that first of all they needed an observatory so that they could set up their telescopes and other instruments, and the king decided they should have one. It was built not far outside Paris, but far enough so that the lights of the city would not interfere with their observations of the stars. Then they went to work.

The first director of the Royal Academy was an Italian astronomer and scientist named Giovanni Domenico Cassini.

When he arrived in Paris he changed his name to Jean Dominique Cassini and became a citizen of France. One of the reasons he was appointed Director of the Academy was that he had studied Galileo's scheme for finding the longitude, and had published a fine set of timetables of the satellites of Jupiter after watching the stars every night for sixteen years. His knowledge would help the other astronomers at the Academy. Louis XIV wanted to have better maps of France, and the only way he could have them was to know more about the longitude and how to find it. He had offered huge rewards to anyone who could find the answer to the problem, but so far he had had no better luck than other kings.

The scientists under Cassini worked on two problems at the same time. One was the perfection of the pendulum clock. The other was the problem of remeasuring the earth so that they would know just how many miles or leagues there were in a degree of latitude or a degree of longitude. While some of them designed and built new and better instruments, others took their telescopes, compasses and other surveying instruments into the country and began to remeasure the circumference of the earth.

The royal surveyors used the same scheme for measuring the world that the ancients used. But instead of guessing the distance between two places, they measured every foot of it on the ground with the best instruments that had ever been built. And instead of guessing that two cities were located on a north-south line, they set up instruments including telescopes, and surveyed a long "base line" that ran exactly north and south. This first survey took two years, and when it was finished

149

and all the figures had been worked out, the final measurement of the circumference of the earth was remarkably accurate. And with their figures, the scientists fixed the value of a degree of arc around the circle of the earth in terms of miles or leagues or any other kind of linear measure.

This gentleman surveyor of four hundred years ago rode in style. A dial attached to the wheels of his carriage measured the miles. His assistant sketched the road and the countryside as they traveled along.

All this time work was going ahead on the determination of longitude between two places far apart. The planet Jupiter and the timetables of Cassini were the answer — at least on land — and it was a scheme that was used by all nations for the next two hundred and fifty years.

The scientists of the Academy drew a map twenty-four feet

in diameter on the floor of the observatory of Paris. It was an unusual map, because it was a map drawn as though you were looking down at the earth from the sky with the North Pole in the center. The lands below the equator were squeezed up towards the equator, but they were all there. Out from the center they drew meridians of longitude equally spaced so that they spread across the map like the spokes of a wheel. Then the astronomers began to plot the true longitudes of places around the globe and put them on the map where they belonged.

Many expeditions were sent out from Paris to all parts of the world. The astronomers and surveyors carried with them telescopes, quadrants, and pendulum clocks that would keep very accurate time. They also carried with them copies of Cassini's timetables of the eclipses of the satellites of Jupiter. The French astronomers corresponded with astronomers in all parts of the earth. They sent them the timetables of Jupiter and all the information they could give them about how to find the longitude. Letters came to Paris from astronomers in parts of Siam, and China; cities such as Mexico City, London, Quebec, and many other places. People everywhere were studying astronomy and the planet Jupiter. And every time some new information came in about the longitude of a place, it was marked on the big map on the floor of the Paris observatory. In a very few years the map of the world looked a lot different, and people knew a lot more about its size and the actual distances between places from east to west than they had ever known before.

chapter 2

John Harrison's
Clock

All the world admitted that the French Royal Academy of Sciences was doing a wonderful service by helping map makers find the longitude in different parts of the world. But there was still one great problem to be solved: how could navigators find their longitude in the middle of the ocean? The giant pendulum clocks or "regulators" that were used in the observatories could not be carried out to sea, and no one had invented a clock of any kind that would stand the rough treatment it would have to take on board a ship and still keep accurate time.

If a timekeeper of some kind was the answer to finding the longitude at sea it would have to be very accurate indeed and very sturdy. According to the figures that scientists had worked out, a degree of longitude at the equator was equal to about sixty-eight miles, or four minutes by the clock. One minute of time by the clock meant seventeen miles — towards or away from a dangerous coast line or a pile of rocks. And if a navigator on a long ocean voyage wanted to find his longitude within half a degree (thirty-four miles), his timekeeper must not gain or lose more than two minutes in forty-two days, or *three seconds a day.* Many people felt that it would be impossible to build any kind of clock that would keep that kind of time, especially if it was going to be tossed around in a rolling ship in a bad storm. But there was a solution to the problem, and it came from England. So did the clock that solved it.

King Charles II of England built an astronomical observatory in Greenwich Park, overlooking the Thames River. He did just about what Louis XIV did in France. His astronomers worked hard on the same problems the French were working on. King Charles also offered a huge reward to anyone who could figure out a way of finding the longitude at sea, because many of his ships were being lost. Both merchant seamen and naval officers were desperate for some method of finding their longitude, and loud complaints were coming in from the waterfront. In 1690 war broke out between England and France, and the English fleet was badly defeated at the battle of Beachy Head. The next year several English ships were lost off the coast of Plymouth because they could not get their bearings, that is, find their latitude and longitude. Several years later four of His Majesty's ships and two thousand men were lost when the fleet ran on the rocks off the southwest coast of England. The situation was serious and the government was determined to do something about it.

In 1713 England's Parliament passed a bill "providing publick reward for such person or persons as shall discover the longitude." It was a desperate appeal, the result of many costly disasters at sea and the pressure from other countries who were constantly challenging England's best efforts to secure her maritime supremacy. Therefore, Parliament stood ready to pay for any practical invention the sums of:

Ten thousand pounds for any device that would determine longitude within one degree (4 minutes of time, or 68 miles)

John Harrison's prize-winning marine chronometer, "No. 4," which solved the problem of determining longitude at sea.

Fifteen thousand pounds for any device that would determine the longitude within forty minutes of arc (approximately 45 miles)

Twenty thousand pounds for any device that would determine the longitude within 30 minutes (2 minutes of time, or 34 miles).

As though aware of the absurdity of their terms, Parliament authorized the formation of a permanent commission — the Board of Longitude — and empowered it to pay smaller rewards for any practical inventions which showed promise, even though they failed to meet the rigid standards attached to the grand prize. For fifty years this handsome reward stood untouched, a prize for the impossible, the butt of English comedians and cartoonists. The Board of Longitude, hounded by fools and quacks, failed to see the joke. Neither the Board nor anyone else knew exactly what kind of an invention they were looking for, but they did know that for centuries the longitude problem had stopped the best scientific minds of Europe.

By 1715, every physical principle and mechanical part that would have to be incorporated in an accurate timekeeper was understood by watchmakers. All that remained was to bridge the gap between a good clock and one that was nearly perfect. It was that half degree of longitude, that two minutes of time, that meant the difference between conquest and failure, the difference between twenty thousand pounds and just another timekeeper.

The longitude problem was solved, finally, by a ticking engine in a box, the invention of an uneducated Yorkshire carpenter named John Harrison. The device was the marine chronometer.

John Harrison was born in Foulby in the parish of Wragby, Yorkshire, in May, 1693, the son of a carpenter and joiner. He began to play with watches when he was six years old and was convalescing from a case of smallpox. He learned his father's trade, but most of his spare time was spent reading published lectures on physics and mathematics and books on watchmaking. In 1715, when he was twenty-two, he built his first grandfather clock, or regulator.

All of the wheels except the escape wheel were hand-carved, teeth and all, from oak. Not satisfied with the going of his clock or of any other clocks, for that matter, young Harrison spent many hours studying their mechanical defects and possible ways of correcting them.

Weather was the curse of clockmakers; sudden changes of temperature made metal parts expand or contract. Harrison invented a "gridiron" pendulum of nine alternating steel and brass rods so pinned together that expansion or contraction caused by variation in temperature was eliminated, the unlike rods counteracting each other. He also devised an ingenious "escapement," the piece which releases for a second, more or less, the driving force of a timekeeper, such as a suspended weight or a coiled mainspring. This "grasshopper" escapement, nearly frictionless and noiseless, required no lubrication. Equipped with this ingenious gadget, one of his early grandfather clocks ran without gaining or losing more than a second a month during a period of fourteen years.

Harrison was twenty years old when Parliament posted the

twenty-thousand-pound reward for a method of determining longitude at sea. Certainly the young clockmaker must have been aware of such a fabulous reward and one so widely advertised. Yet it was 1728, after he had built his first two fine grandfather clocks, before Harrison, then thirty-five, ventured forth to London with his plans for a marine timekeeper. He carried with him full-scale models of his gridiron pendulum and his grasshopper escapement, and was prepared to face the awe-inspiring Board of Longitude. But before he reached them he was advised by Edmund Halley, Astronomer Royal, and George Graham, England's leading clock expert, not to apply for funds for research, but to build his timekeeper and then apply for a chance at the prize money.

Harrison went home and spent the next seven years fashioning a timekeeper that would meet the specifications of the Board of Longitude. With infinite patience he struggled to overcome friction in all moving parts, and to counteract the effects of sharp changes in temperature. In 1735 he finished the job and came up with an amazingly accurate timekeeper, but one that was heavy and cumbersome. It weighed seventy-two pounds, and its two huge balances weighed five pounds apiece. Mounted in gimbals that allowed it to swing in any direction, it was tested unofficially on a barge in the Humber River. Its performance was much better than its appearance. Five members of the Royal Society put their stamp of approval on the machine, and on the strength of their report, the Board of Longitude in 1736 arranged for a trial of the clock at sea aboard H.M.S. *Centurion,* Captain Proctor, bound out for Lisbon.

Captain Proctor gave Harrison the run of the ship, and his huge timekeeper was set up in the captain's own cabin, where it could be tended and wound without interference. The ship's officers were courteous but skeptical. No record of the clock's going on the outward passage is known, but on the return run in H.M.S. *Orford*, Captain Man, the skipper, stated that "When we made the land, the said land, according to my reckoning (and others), ought to have been The Start; but before we knew what land it was, John Harrison declared to me and the rest of the ship's company, that according to his observations with his machine, it ought to be The Lizard — the which, indeed, it was found to be, his observation showing the ship to be more west than my reckoning, above one degree and twenty-six miles." It is interesting that even on this well-worn trade route it was not considered a scandal that the ship's navigator should make an error of ninety miles in his landfall.

After examining the affidavit of Captain Man, the Board of Longitude awarded Harrison five hundred pounds towards the expense of building a second, more compact, machine "in the nature of clockwork," which machine was to be delivered into the hands of His Majesty's ship's captains when completed. Harrison finished "Number Two" in 1739, a much-improved machine with brass wheels instead of wood; but it was even more awkward to handle than Number One, weighing one hundred and three pounds, and its case and gimbal suspension weighing another sixty-two pounds. Harrison tested it himself for nearly two years, under conditions of "great heat and motion," but it was never sent to sea, because at that time

England was at war with Spain and the Admiralty had no desire to give the Spaniards a chance to capture it.

While he was testing Number Two, Harrison went to work on a third timekeeper, and in 1741 the Board of Longitude voted him another five hundred pounds, enough to keep him from starving to death. Harrison felt sure he could perfect Number Three in a short time and have the thing ready for a sea test by August of 1741, but five years later he was still struggling with the new clock balance he had devised for his third timekeeper.

By this time Harrison had received several small grants from the Board of Longitude, and his fame as a master craftsman was spreading. Even the Royal Society was impressed by his skill and patience. Because of his extreme modesty they forgot, at least for a time, his lack of academic background and awarded him their Copley medal, the highest honor they could give a man.

Convinced that Number Three would never satisfy him, Harrison began work on Number Four and Number Five even before Number Three was tested at sea. He was then sixty-four years old. Number Four resembled an enormous "pair-case" watch about five inches in diameter, complete with pendant. The dial was white enamel with an ornamental design in black. Instead of a gimbal suspension, Harrison used nothing but a plain box and a soft cushion to transport his clock, which, as one writer said, "by reason alike of its beauty, its accuracy, and its historical interest, must take pride of place as the most famous chronometer that ever has been or ever will be made." The pivot holes were jeweled to the third wheel with rubies and

159

the end stones were diamonds. After fifty years of unremitting toil, Harrison himself felt safe in saying that "there is neither any other mechanical or mathematical thing in the world that is more beautiful or curious in texture than this my watch or Timekeeper for the longitude . . . and I heartily thank Almighty God that I have lived so long, as in some measure to complete it."

In 1761, after testing Number Four for two years, a trial at sea was arranged, and because of his poor health, John Harrison, then sixty-eight, appointed his son William to make the trip to Jamaica aboard H.M.S. *Deptford,* whose captain was Dudley Digges. After many delays the *Deptford* sailed on November 18 from Spithead with a convoy, after first touching at Portland and Plymouth.

Number Four was placed in a wooden case with four locks, and it could not be wound or touched without four men being present: young Harrison, Governor Lyttleton of Jamaica, Captain Digges and his first lieutenant. Meanwhile the Board of Longitude had arranged to have the longitude of Jamaica recalculated for this test by observing the eclipses of Jupiter's satellites with telescopes. The difference in mean or local time between Jamaica and Portsmouth, England, was to be determined by Harrison's timekeeper and checked against the observations.

Nine days out from Plymouth all hands were alerted lest the ship overrun Madeira. By dead reckoning the *Deptford* was then 13° 50′ west of Greenwich, but according to Harrison's timekeeper she was 15° 19′ W. Young Harrison told the skipper that Madeira would be sighted the next day. Although Captain

Digges offered to bet Harrison five to one that he was wrong, he held his course, and sure enough, at 6 A.M. the next morning the lookout sighted Porto Santo, in the Madeira islands, dead ahead.

At Jamaica, Number Four was taken ashore and checked for accuracy. After allowing for its rate of going (2⅔ seconds a day losing at Portsmouth) it was found to be five seconds slow, an error in longitude of 1¼ minutes only, or 1¼ nautical miles. On the return trip to England the weather was very rough and Number Four took an unmerciful pounding, despite the fact that young Harrison tended it carefully. Yet when the clock was checked again at Portsmouth its total error for the five months' voyage was only one minute and 53½ seconds of time, or 28½ minutes of longitude — safely within the limit of the half a degree required to win the prize of twenty thousand pounds.

Instead of reaping the reward and enjoying his rightful hour of triumph for a lifetime of work, John Harrison was immediately beset by troubles. He had mastered the longitude, but he did not know how to cope with the Board of Longitude or his competitors in the Royal Society. A few of the members wanted very much to win the prize of twenty thousand pounds, and one or two of them had spent large sums of their own money developing other methods of finding the longitude. So it was that when the Board of Longitude gave their opinion, they decided that the remarkable performance of Harrison's timekeeper must be a fluke; they said they had never been allowed to see the mechanism, and besides, if a hundred clocks were transported to Jamaica under the same conditions, one

161

or more out of the lot might perform equally well — at least for one voyage.

The Board gave Harrison another reward of two thousand five hundred pounds and Parliament passed an Act (February 1763) granting him five thousand pounds as soon as he should tell them the secret of his invention, something he stoutly refused to do. Meanwhile the Board granted him a new trial for his timekeeper at sea. Number Four was to be checked at the Royal Observatory at Greenwich before sailing, but Harrison balked. He said that he did not care to let his clock out of his hands until he had reaped some profit from it. But he did agree to send his own rating of the clock's behavior, sealed, to the Secretary of the Admiralty before the trial began.

After endless delays William Harrison embarked with Number Four in H.M.S. *Tartar,* Captain Sir John Lindsay, this time bound out for the island of Barbados. The second trial was the same story all over again. On April 18, twenty-one days out, young Harrison took two altitudes of the sun at noon to get his latitude, and announced to Sir John that they were forty-three miles east of Porto Santo. The captain accordingly steered a direct course for it, and at one o'clock the next morning the island was sighted, "which exactly agreed with the Distance mentioned above." Day after day young Harrison plotted the position of the ship according to the time kept by Number Four, and on May 12, at eleven o'clock at night, he told the captain that according to his reckoning they were about eight or nine miles from land. Sir John decided to lay to rather than risk running aground, and sure enough, at daybreak Barbados was sighted on the horizon.

JOHN HARRISON'S CLOCK

From Portsmouth to Barbados, a seven weeks' voyage, Number Four showed an error of 38.4 seconds or 9.6 miles of longitude at the equator. Checked again at Portsmouth when the trial was over, Number Four had gained (after allowing for its daily rate of going) a total of 54 seconds over a period of 156 days. If further allowance were made for change of rate caused by variations in temperature, information posted beforehand by John Harrison, the rate of Number Four would have been reduced to an error of 15 seconds of loss in five months, or *less than a tenth of a second a day.*

The evidence in favor of Harrison's chronometer was overwhelming, and could no longer be ignored or set aside. But the Board of Longitude was not through. They admitted that this strange timekeeper had kept the longitude well within limits, but they also said that in order to receive the balance of the first ten thousand pounds prize money Harrison would have to turn over to them complete working drawings of his clock and also demonstrate to the Board the operation and construction of each part, including the process he used to temper the springs. And finally, he was to turn over to the Board of Longitude all four of his timekeepers.

Harrison was disappointed and bitter. "I hope I am the first," he wrote, "and for my country's sake, shall be the last that suffers by pinning my faith on an English Act of Parliament." The public became interested in his troubles, and his friends launched a publicity campaign against the Board of Longitude. As a result the Board gave in and finally authorized payment of the balance of the first ten thousand pounds of his reward. The second half did not come so easily.

Harrison had now taken his clock apart before witnesses and demonstrated its mechanism. He had then turned it over to the Board of Longitude, and by them it was held in trust for the people of England. It was carefully guarded against prying eyes and tampering. Yet somehow a set of plans, based on Harrison's own drawings, was engraved and published without his permission. The unpaid balance of the reward was his, and he could not collect it. Harrison wrote that he and his son had so far been paid for their years of labor at a rate no better than "common Mechanicks." There were other sorry experiences. Number Four was carried to the Royal Observatory at Greenwich where it was put through a series of exhaustive tests. It would seem that every effort was made to find some fault with it. A duplicate of Number Four was ordered by the Board, to be made by Larcum Kendall, England's most famous clockmaker. Meanwhile Harrison was instructed to produce a Number Five and Number Six, and these were to undergo exhaustive tests before the balance of the prize money would be paid. Yet he was not permitted to borrow Number Four to use as a pattern for Five and Six.

John Harrison was now seventy-eight years old. His eyes were failing and his hands were not as steady as they had been. Fortunately one of his great admirers was none other than His Majesty George III, who had already granted Harrison and his son an audience. So it was that Harrison finally appealed to his king in person and when "Farmer George" had heard his story he vowed that the Harrisons would receive their just dues. The king resolved to appear before the Bar of the House of Commons, if necessary, and testify in Harrison's behalf. At this

164

point the Board of Longitude began to squirm. They made one last attempt to make William Harrison consent to new trials and new conditions, but father and son stood fast. Meanwhile, with pressure from the king and public indignation behind them, Parliament drew up a money bill in record time; the king gave it the nod and it was passed. The Harrisons had won their fight and their prize.

chapter X.

To Map
a Nation

Few countries in the world are islands completely surrounded
by water. Most of them have neighbors on all sides, and the
boundary lines between them are shared. Therefore, when a
national boundary line is changed, the neighbors have something to say about where it is going to be moved. It is not
enough for a nation to tell a neighbor that if the boundary line
between them is moved the maps of both countries will be
more accurate. One or the other is going to lose some land, and
no one ever wants to lose land.

Three hundred years ago in Europe every national boundary
needed to be remeasured and most of them needed to be moved
in one direction or another. The trouble was that as soon as
one country started to move its boundary lines, all the others
would have to do the same thing, and at the same time. It
would be a kind of chain reaction. Some countries would gain
a little more land and others would lose some. For this reason
all eyes turned to France when she began to make plans for a
new and accurate map of her territory. And as soon as the
scientists at the French Academy of Sciences started to make
new surveys and measurements across the country, every other

166

nation in Europe began to move and measure, just to make sure the neighbors did not trespass or try to claim more land than they owned. Although France started this great reform of geography and map making, other nations were not far behind.

By the year 1700 almost every nation in Europe realized how important it was to have good national maps as well as an accurate map of the whole of Europe. And by that time all the tools and instruments that are used today in map making and surveying had been invented. Most of them were very accurate. There were fine quadrants and sextants for the measurement of latitudes. There were accurate timetables of the sun and stars, made by the astronomers in the great observatories. And there were pendulum clocks that could be carried from place to place for the measurement of longitude. Having all this fine apparatus to work with, map makers had only one thing left to do, and that was to go out into the field and make new measurements and new maps. They were ready and willing, but there had to be someone who would pay the bills, because map making has always been an expensive job. For this reason national maps, almost from the very beginning, were paid for by national governments.

In France, Louis XIV and his minister, Jean Colbert, were quite willing to pay for a new map of the country. Colbert thought that the lack of an accurate map of the kingdom of France was a national disgrace. A large-scale map of the country, he said, was as important in peace time as it was in fighting a war. It would help to locate and describe the natural resources of the country that many a Frenchman knew nothing about. And if France had to fight a war it would make clear to everyone the land they were fighting about. Colbert told the scientists at the Royal Academy that he would find the money. He also promised them his full support, and to prove that he meant what he said, written orders went out to all the provinces of France, instructing the local politicians and other men in authority to give the surveyors all the help they needed. Soon after that the job was started.

Out went the surveyors, taking with them all their instruments including their big pendulum clocks. They crisscrossed the whole country. Everywhere they stopped they set up their instruments and figured out the exact latitude and longitude of the place. And each time they made their measurements they found serious mistakes on the old maps that needed to be corrected.

It was slow work mapping the entire country. For ten years the surveyors plodded along through swamps and forests, getting cold and wet and very tired. And as the work went on the surveyors and Jean Colbert wondered whether next year there would be enough money in the royal treasury to finish the job. Finally the survey was finished, and for the first time in history France had a map dotted with cities and towns, rivers and hills, that were just where they ought to be. Everyone agreed that the time and labor, not to mention the money, were well spent, and that at last France had a map to be proud of.

Everyone was pleased with the result. The new map was printed on one sheet, and when it was placed on top of the old ones that Frenchmen had depended on for years, the country had a new look. The coast lines on the west had shrunk in some places and bulged in others. All across the country latitudes and longitudes had been shifted in one direction or another. In some places the changes did not amount to a great deal, but in others distances were corrected by as much as a hundred miles. This first map of France was not much more than an outline, but it was accurate, and by using it as a guide,

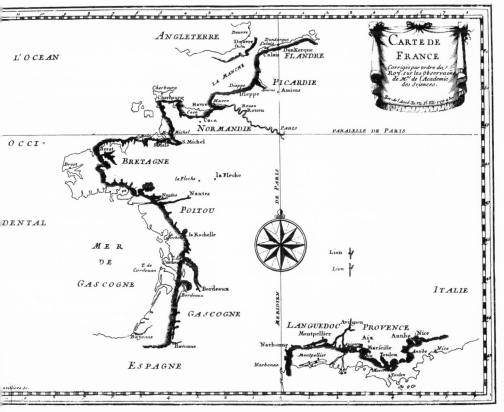

The new outline of France (shaded) was a much better picture of the country than the old ones used for hundreds of years.

169

Triangulation in France (above). Picard's meridian line (below).

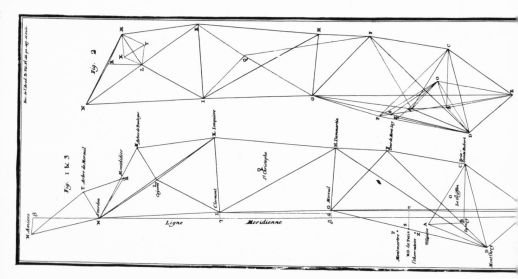

topographical engineers were able to go over the same ground again, filling in such details as small streams, bridges, low hills and valleys. This final polishing took many years and millions of dollars.

Scientists all over the world had watched what was going on in France. Many of them visited the observatory in Paris and studied the methods and instruments that were being used in the mapping of the country. But not all the visitors were scientists. The Czar of Russia heard about the Royal Academy of France and took a long trip to Paris in order to see what was going on there. He wanted to meet some of the map makers who were said to be the best in France, if not the world. He wanted to find out whether they could tell him more than he already knew about his own country, the land of the Muscovites. In Paris the Czar met and talked with many men, but he was especially interested in the brothers Delisle: Guillaume, Joseph and Louis. They might be able to help him find out how much land Russia owned and what it might be good for. Shortly after he got home from Paris, Peter the Great and his wife Catherine invited Joseph and Louis Delisle to come to Russia and organize a school of astronomy and at the same time teach Russian engineers how to make maps of their own country.

The Delisle brothers finally accepted the invitation. In Russia they were treated handsomely, and in their turn they proved to be ambassadors of good will as well as technical advisers. They organized a school of astronomy. They prepared a textbook for students. They taught young men how to build telescopes and other instruments, and at the end of each school term they distributed prizes to the best students in the school. The Delisles also worked hard in the field, exploring all parts of Muscovy. They made long, dangerous journeys far into the interior, where even the Russians themselves had done very little exploring. These two men and their helpers tackled the same job in Russia that was being done in France. But in Russia the winters were long and cold, and the country was wild.

Louis Delisle explored the coast of the Arctic Ocean, Lapland and Archangel, making observations and measurements wherever he stopped. He crossed Siberia as far as the peninsula of Kamchatka. From there he set sail with Vitus Bering, the great explorer. But the bitter cold and the hard work were too much for Delisle. He died of exposure a few months later. His brother Joseph spent twenty-two years in Russia, and when he went home to France he carried with him hundreds of maps and charts as well as thousands of pages of notes about the country that he and his brother had written. All this material added up to the first detailed report to reach Europe about one of the strangest and most faraway places in the world, a region about which Europeans knew almost nothing. It was a priceless geographical treasure.

The survey of Russia by French scientists was the beginning of international co-operation on a world-wide project. It also proved how important it was for all nations to work together and share their geographical knowledge. No nation could work alone if the whole world was to be remapped, and all scientists and many kings were ready to admit it.

Before many years international co-operation among scientists moved westward across the English Channel to the British Isles. English astronomers and map makers were hard at work in the great observatory at Greenwich, carefully measuring the latitudes and longitudes of places in all parts of their country. They had established a prime meridian of longitude through their observatory and were making measurements east and west of it. At the same time the French were making their measurements through the observatory at Paris. Both countries realized that if the difference in longitude between the two observatories could be accurately measured, the map of France and the map of the British Isles could be linked together. It would be a fine start for a new map of Europe. In 1783 the British government received a polite letter from France inviting her neighbors to make a joint survey of the longitude between the Paris observatory and the one at Greenwich. The invitation was promptly accepted, and both countries began to work together.

This early perambulator (odometer) clicked off the miles as it was wheeled along the ground. Today the same instrument is attached to the side of an automobile for the same purpose.

173

A night scene in an early observatory. The man sitting on the floor is peering at a star through his telescope. The man at the right is timing the passing of the star.

Up to that time no surveying had been attempted over such long distances or across a body of water as broad as the English Channel. In order to do it, the English first made a careful survey from Greenwich down to the Channel coast. At the

A view of the Royal Observatory at Greenwich, 1785.

174

The Observatory of Paris, 1785, from the rear.

same time the French surveyed the distance from the Paris observatory to the western coast of France. Then the trick was to connect the two measurements by jumping the English Channel. The job was done at night with the help of powerful lights that served as points to sight at and signals for the surveyors on both coasts. Some of the lights were steady beams of white, and others were blinkers that could flash signals back and forth.

The problem was simple enough — to measure a series of great triangles across the water, a process called "triangulation," depending on the magic of geometry to provide the answer and the distance, for if the length of one leg of a triangle and two of its angles are known, the length of its other two sides can be figured out without any trouble. It was an old method of measuring land, used by surveyors for thousands

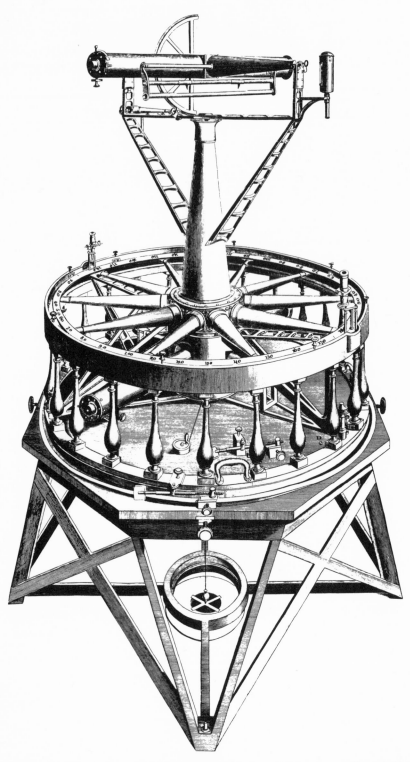

Jesse Ramsden's theodolite, built for the Royal Society, made possible the first accurate triangulation of England.

of years, and it still worked. But in the case of measuring the distance across the English Channel there was one important difference. The two principal triangles were big. The length of one leg of one of the triangles was forty-seven miles, and another leg turned out to be forty-eight miles. But with the help of lights and a very accurate instrument to measure the angles between the signal lights on both shores, the scientists on both sides of the Channel did an almost perfect job.

After this first cross-Channel survey was made, England went on about the business of making an accurate and detailed map of herself and all the British Isles. Like the surveyors of France, the English had their troubles — finding the money to carry on an expensive project and convincing the people of the country that an accurate map of the land was worth the price and the small tax they might have to pay to have the maps published. However, every year the national survey became more expensive to operate, and finally the British army took over the responsibility of mapping the country, accurately and on a large scale.

The project became known as the Ordnance Survey, and it was organized as a separate department of the British government. The Ordnance Survey maps are probably the most famous in the world. Even the first sheets were amazing. Two hundred and eighteen stations were set up across Great Britain and Ireland for the use of surveyors, and 1554 bearings, or points, were established all over the country with permanent markers set in the ground. The precise latitude and longitude of each point was recorded for future reference and as an official standard for surveyors to work from.

Pl. IX.   PLAN of the TRIANGLES whereby the DISTANCE between the

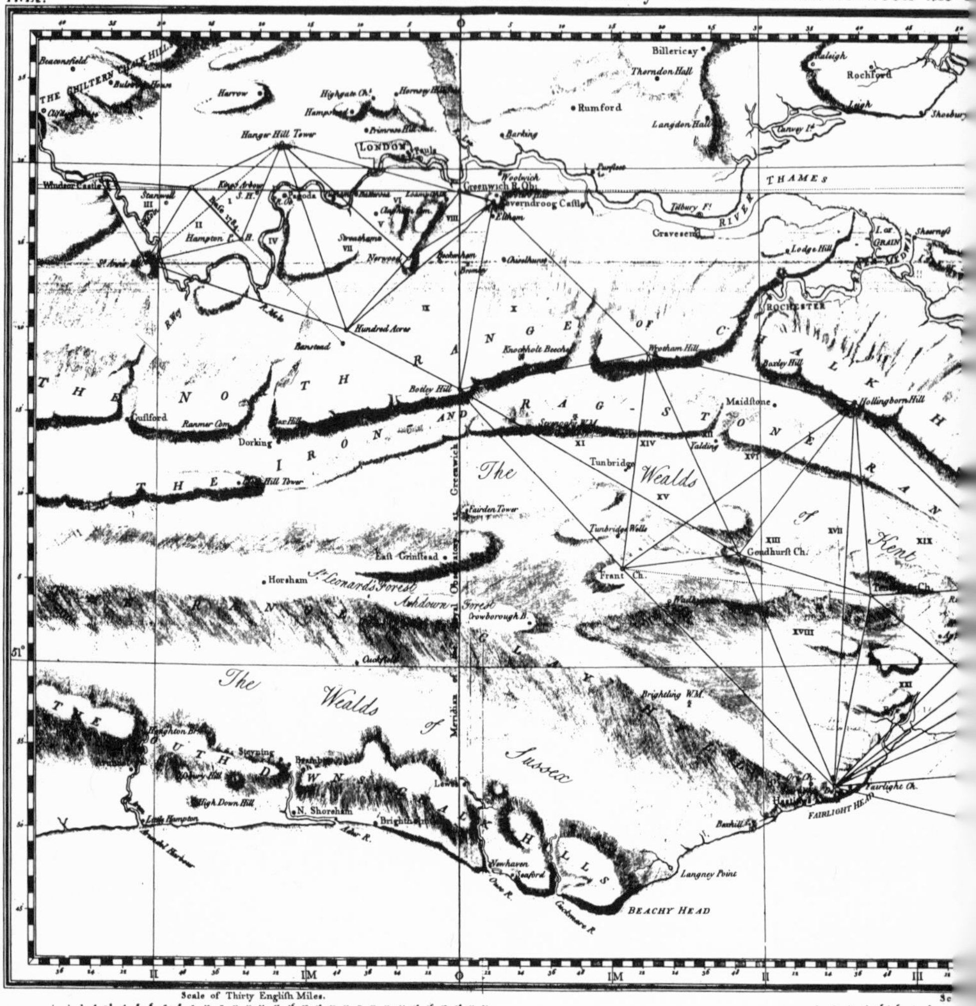

Scale of Thirty English Miles.

Philos. Trans. Vol. LXXX. Tab. XIII. p. 172.

Parallel of Greenwich R. Ob. Lat. 51. 28. 40.

Perpendicular to the Meridian of Greenwich R. Ob.

NORTH FORELAND

Margate
St Peters
or THANET
Ramsgate

Sandwich

Deal
Walmer Castle

Waldershare Mon.
Light Ho. SOUTH FORELAND

Dover Castle

Folkstone

Meridian of the Royal Observatory at Paris

Dunes

French Fort
Fort Reveau
Dunkirk XLIII

Hondscote

XLV

XXXVI
Gravelines
XLII

Blancnez
Calais
XL
XLI

CAPE BLANCNEZ
Blancnez Sig.
XXXV
XXXVIII
XXXIX
Broukeek

CAPE GRISNEZ
XXXIII
Whtton
Mont Cassel

Boule
Montlambert Sig.

Scale of Thirty Thousand Toises, Ratio to the Fathoms as 1065.75 to 1000.

The English Channel between England and France. The
lines across the water show the way surveyors measured the
distance between the observatories at Greenwich, England,
and Paris, France.

By the year 1900 the Ordnance Survey was far different from the way it had been at the beginning of the project. The original plan was to make a map on about one hundred sheets that would cost the government about twenty thousand dollars. But every year the project and the budget grew. By 1851, the Ordnance Survey had become such an important part of English life — its government, its military forces and its people — that the budget was increased to more than a million dollars. And instead of making one hundred map sheets, the first complete survey map was printed on 108,000 sheets. These were drawn on several different scales so that the map would be helpful to many people in different occupations and with different interests. The plans of cities and towns, for example, were made on a very large scale, so that the map of the metropolitan area of London alone, made up from separate sheets, was about three hundred feet long and two hundred feet wide when the sheets were pasted together.

The first great maps of France and Great Britain did much more than give those two countries an accurate picture of themselves, for while the work was in progress the outside world watched and waited and learned. Other nations began to realize the importance of good maps and charts and their relation to good government. Not only governments began to see the light, but private citizens as well. The merchant and manufacturer, the farmer and the professional man began to think of maps in terms of prosperity and security instead of just another burden to be carried by the taxpayer. Government surveyors who walked over a person's land began to be respected and appreciated as people who were trying to improve the community instead of being thought of as trespassers against the personal rights and civil liberties of the small landholder. Taxpayers stopped complaining, because on some of the large-scale sheets of the Ordnance map a person could sometimes find his own home, the lane that led up to it and the little stream where he liked to go fishing.

Every country that tackled a national mapping program ran into trouble, but none of them had as many problems to solve as Switzerland, an up and down country. And because she was able to solve her mapping problems, Switzerland made a most important contribution to the science of map making, by showing the world how to draw mountains and valleys on a map.

An ordinary map of Switzerland meant nothing to the people who lived there or anyone else. Distances from place to place could be figured out in terms of latitude and longitude, the way the crow flies, but that is not the way people travel in Switzerland. Around every turn in the road they go up or they go down. Whether they are walking or riding they go up and down more than they go ahead. For this reason Switzerland, one of the most beautiful countries in the world, presented a challenge to artists, map makers and surveyors, and a problem that was hard to solve.

The first man who tried to make a map of the country gave it up as a bad job. He filled his drawing with pretty pictures of castles, monasteries, churches and other prominent buildings. Then, in order to tell his readers something about the topography of the country, he drew long chains of lumps or molehills that were supposed to represent hills and mountains.

Other map makers tried to make a good map of the country, but most of them failed.

A sensible and accurate map of Switzerland spelled trouble for surveyors as well as map makers. It meant inventing some way of showing artistically and clearly the high mountains and deep valleys that cover the entire country. Therefore, it is no wonder that it took so many years for Switzerland to produce her first national map.

The first accurate map of Switzerland was begun in 1830, under the direction of General Dufour, and after twelve years of hard work the first sheet was printed and published. Thirty-four years later the whole map was finished. It was different from any map the world had ever seen. It was accurate, so far as latitudes and longitudes were concerned, but more than that it was artistic. Dufour and his men tried to show the country as it really was, with all its mountains and valleys. And he did it by shading the colors he used, and with contour lines, wavy lines that told people whether they were looking at a mountain 15,000 feet high or the flat land at the bottom of a valley. His map was as close as he could come to a photographic picture of the country, and it told the story. He showed other map makers how color could be used to indicate whether the land was high or low, and how contour lines with numbers on them could be used to tell just how high the mountain was. The completed map of Switzerland covered more than five hundred sheets. Looking at any one of these sheets, the reader has the feeling that he is looking down on the country from an airplane.

The mapping of America is a long story, enough to fill a book or two. The first maps of the New World were made even before Columbus discovered America. They were made by people who just guessed that there were other lands on the opposite side of the globe that could be found if someone had the courage to sail far enough to the west. And after 1492 hundreds of maps were published to show the people of Europe the great wide world that had been discovered across the Atlantic Ocean. Most of these early maps were very crude, in many cases made by people who did not know what they were talking about. A few were fairly accurate, but these were maps of a very small area, maps made by surveyors who actually saw and measured the land. But whether these early maps were accurate or not, they are all part of a fascinating story — the story of how America and the United States finally got on the map for the first time.

The United States was officially born in 1783, when a treaty was signed between the British Empire and the American colonies that had decided to become an independent nation. And at that time no nation in the world was less sure of her boundary lines than the United States of America. But for a few years after the country was born, no person was interested in maps or boundary lines. Everyone in the new nation was tired after fighting the long Revolutionary War. The government was new and inexperienced and there was almost no money in the national treasury. For these reasons many important projects had to wait for a while, including a national map.

Scientific mapping in the United States began just after the purchase of Louisiana in 1803. Louisiana was a broad territory that stretched westward far over the horizon. No one knew just how far, and few people cared. Most of the citizens of the

Ohio River

Orleans

chase

Thomas Jefferson negotiated it, the United States bought the land and off the country marched towards the West Coast.

United States were not much interested in the wilds of North America that lay to the west of the Mississippi River. There was plenty of land for everyone to the east of the Great River, and no sane person would want to settle beyond it. People had heard too many stories about wild Indians, deserts, rattlesnakes and land that was good for nothing. However, not everyone felt the same way.

One of the people who believed in the future growth and development of the United States, both east and west of the Mississippi River, was Thomas Jefferson. In 1796 he made a speech to his fellow scientists in the American Philosophical Society at Philadelphia. He pointed out to them that whether the United States purchased Louisiana or not, it was important to explore that great territory west of the Mississippi. Some of the scientists agreed with him and others did not. But after four years, Jefferson became President of the United States, and from then on he had the power to do a great many things he could not do as a private citizen.

As soon as the purchase of Louisiana was made, President Jefferson went into action. He talked Congress into giving him a special grant of money for the purpose of exploring the new territory. Then he appointed two able men to lead an expedition west of the Mississippi River. One was Meriwether Lewis, Jefferson's private secretary, and the other was Captain William Clark of the United States Army. Their instructions came from the President himself. They were to explore the new territory and survey a route from the Mississippi River to the Pacific Ocean, and to learn as much as they could about the country as they went along.

The Lewis and Clark expedition was a great success, and it was just the beginning. From then on, hardly a year went by without at least one military surveying party being sent into the field to carry on the job. Yet in spite of all the interesting discoveries that were made by these surveying parties, many citizens still had their doubts about the West. The country was so big, and so much of it was not fit to live in, according to reports, that it did not seem worth while to spend a lot of the taxpayers' money surveying it, or trying to map it as carefully as some of the countries of Europe had been mapped. For this reason it took many years and many changes in people's thinking before Congress was willing to appropriate money to begin work on a national map of the United States. And even after the first appropriation was made, many people in the government were not sure just what department should have charge of the operation.

In spite of the fact that some congressional delegates believed that the mapping of the whole country was going to be a terrible waste of money, President Jefferson wanted very much to make a start. In 1807 he suggested to Congress that they appropriate enough money to begin a survey of the Atlantic Coast, so that navigators would know where they were going and where they were at any time. Congress approved of the idea, and that same year an official "Survey of the Coast" was organized. This new branch of the government was placed under the direction of the Treasury Department, and a Swiss scientist and map maker named Ferdinand Hassler was appointed to direct the job.

The Survey of the Coast grew slowly. It took Americans a

long time to find out how important it was to have accurate charts of the 100,000 miles of coastline that belonged to the United States. In 1843 the department was reorganized and placed under the direction of the Navy Department. It was renamed and called the United States Coast and Geodetic Survey. Its surveyors branched out from the coast and made observations of latitudes and longitudes all the way across the country. They also made many beautiful maps and charts. Today the Coast and Geodetic Survey does much more than publish maps. It publishes *Coast Pilots,* books that describe in words the dangers that a ship's captain may run into along the coasts of the United States. It also publishes lists describing the lighthouses and buoys that are placed along the coast to keep sailors out of trouble.

Almost as old as the Coast and Geodetic Survey is the Corps of Topographical Engineers. This was an outfit that grew out of the expedition of Lewis and Clark. It was organized officially in 1813, and in time it became the Corps of Engineers of the War Department. The men in the Corps were army engineers, and all of them had been taught how to make good maps. The Corps of Engineers had many duties. It was supposed to explore the country and map the mountains and valleys, the courses of important rivers and any other things that might be useful to know about in case of war. The Corps of Engineers had its troubles, too. The people who lived and hunted out in the wilderness, both white men and red, needed discipline, and the army engineers were kept so busy making people behave themselves that they did not have time to do much mapping. But these trained men were not lost or forgotten.

In World War II, they were renamed the Army Map Service, one of the most important branches of our armed forces, and one that turned out hundreds of thousands of accurate maps. These maps helped to win the war.

In 1879 the United States government established a third mapping agency. This was named the Geological Survey. Like the first two, the Geological Survey grew up from a small start, and Congress was not sure just what its functions ought to be. But the members of Congress were positive that it was time to find out more about the mineral resources of the country, and the government wanted to know what the country out in the wild West was worth, and how much of the land could be settled and made to pay for itself.

With or without orders, some of the great expeditions that were organized by the Geological Survey began to make the same kind of observations and measurements that the Coast Survey had started many years before. And even though there was no definite plan at the beginning, the Geological Survey began to turn out map sheets on a large scale that were as accurate as any that were being made in Europe, as good as those being made by England's Ordnance Survey. They were so good, in fact, that people from all walks of life began to buy them, and they were used by almost every department of the federal government, just as they are today.

Every year thousands of new maps of the United States, or small parts of it, are published by the United States Government. Many of these maps are made to tell people about special things that a general map does not tell them. More than twenty-seven branches of the government are making maps for themselves and the general public. They publish road surveys, land reclamation maps, forestry maps and many others that have special stories to tell. All of them are useful and we would not know what to do without them. But all of these mapping agencies must thank the three great surveys that first told us about our country — its latitudes, its longitudes, and its natural resources. These were the Coast and Geodetic Survey, the Corps of Engineers, and the Geological Survey.

chapter XII

World
Map Makers

Less than a hundred years ago, within the memory of people now living, there was not a single map of the world in any language that was complete and accurate enough to be called an *international* map. There was no map of the world that any man in any country could read and understand. The different nations of the world were too busy with their own affairs to be bothered with the lands beyond their borders. In addition, they were a little afraid to tackle the big job of making an international map on a large scale. It would be very expensive, and it would mean that many nations would have to forget about war and politics while the map was being made. This was almost too much to ask of human beings who had been quarreling and competing with one another for thousands of years. Most people thought it could not be done at all.

Great progress had been made in the science of map making, but there was still much to be done. As late as 1885 it was estimated that not more than 6,000,000 square miles, less than one ninth of the land surface of the globe, had been surveyed, nor was anyone trying to survey the rest. The remaining eight ninths, inhabited by more than 900,000,000 people, was either unknown or people knew very little about it. A few had seen small pieces of it, perhaps, or they had read a book about foreign lands, but they had not seen a really fine map of the whole world.

The scientists, politicians and military men who thought it would be useful to have some kind of an international map of the world were usually suspected of wanting to spy on their neighbors. Most of the *national* surveys that were being made in the different countries of Europe were under the control of military men who were being paid to defend their countries. Why, then, would it not be dangerous to let them bring their surveyors across national boundary lines and let them discover for themselves the easiest way to invade and conquer their neighbors? National governments thought it would. And so, less than a hundred years ago, the official maps of the various nations of Europe were like the maps of the ancient Egyptians, the Greeks, the Romans and the Phoenicians. They were secret documents that were carefully guarded by the national government. In wartime very few people could even look at them.

In 1885 there were twenty well-organized national surveys being made in different countries of Europe. These were topographic surveys, producing maps of the best quality. Some of the smaller countries of Europe could not afford to survey and map themselves on such a large scale, but they could still make maps of a kind. In 1885 thirty-five countries in Europe were busy making geological surveys and maps of their territories. They were finding out about their mineral resources, they were studying and mapping the different kinds of soil, and in general

192

they were discovering what the land could be made to produce. Naturally the best of these geological surveys were made in the countries where the topography had been studied, where measurements of latitude and longitude were the most accurate.

A third kind of national survey supported by public funds had grown up by 1885. This was the Hydrographic Survey: the charting of the coasts and harbors of the world. Nineteen countries had started work on the project. They wanted better charts of their own coasts and harbors, and better charts of the coasts and harbors visited by their merchant fleets in the far corners of the world. The nations who used the ocean highways most, the ones who traded in foreign waters, were more interested than others in having accurate charts of all the ports visited by their ships. It was natural, then, that England, France and Holland should take the lead in making coastal charts which were as accurate as the topographic and geological maps that were being made.

From the very beginning, all men realized that a hydrographic survey of the world could not be made without the help of every seafaring man and every nation whose ships sailed the high seas. There should be no secrets, and no single nation could work alone. The oceans were too big, and the number of coasts and harbors throughout the world were too many. No one nation could chart them, even if it received permission to do so from local governments. But in this case it was not a matter of pooling knowledge and uniting in the common cause of science and map making. It was a union of seafaring men of all nations against the common perils of the briny deep.

The nautical surveyors of the world were a roving lot, working wherever they were allowed to cruise. Sometimes in foreign waters they were protected by the fact that their work would benefit everyone who sailed a ship, and they were therefore permitted to chart the harbors of hostile nations. At other times, when a country did not want to co-operate, it was necessary for the surveying party to have a naval escort to protect them. However, the Hydrographic Survey became an international project to chart the water world, and it represents the first serious attempt of friendly and unfriendly nations to get together on a mapping project for the benefit of all.

It did not take a genius to decide that an international map of the entire world would mean the same kind of co-operation between nations. No one map maker and no one nation could do it alone. Although scientists of different countries exchanged information on astronomy and surveying, the maps of individual countries were all different. The language of the place names, the systems of measurement, the scales and symbols all varied widely from place to place. Sixty years ago, the map maker who wanted to bring together the maps of every country and make them into an atlas of the world was as badly off as Ortelius, who tried it in 1570. And one of his biggest problems was the choice of a prime meridian of longitude, a line somewhere on the face of the earth that all map makers would accept as a standard meridian, and all could use conveniently.

From ancient days to the year 1880, map makers chose their own prime meridian of longitude, the north-south line they would use to measure distances from east to west. They chose one that was close to home or one that they were familiar with. Ptolemy, for example, chose the Fortunate Islands as his prime meridian. He chose them for the simple reason that they were located at the westernmost limit of the habitable world, out beyond the Pillars of Hercules. He decided that meridians of longitude should be reckoned from there, moving eastward to Alexandria and points beyond. He had not seen the islands, of course. Even though they were talked about, no one knew exactly where they were located.

Centuries later the geographers of Europe continued to pick and choose prime meridians to suit themselves. In 1676 John Seller, an English map maker, chose the city of London. And when General Roy began the Ordnance Survey of England he chose the center of the dome of Saint Paul's Cathedral. Years later, after the Royal Observatory at Greenwich was well organized, England's prime meridian was established there. Other popular prime meridians in Europe were Kraków, Copenhagen, Pisa, Rome, Bologna and Rouen. In America the favorite prime meridians were Washington and Philadelphia. There was a great deal of confusion among map makers, because in 1881 there were no less than fourteen different prime meridians being used on national topographic surveys, not to mention the many other mapping projects that were under way.

About the year 1800 a French scientist named Laplace wrote to his friends and fellow workers that it would be a very good idea if all the nations of the world got together and picked a meridian of longitude that everyone could share. He pointed out that people had gotten together in the field of arithmetic and in making up a calendar of the days and years, so why not pick a standard prime meridian from which all longitudes could be measured, and measured with the same yardstick.

Scientists in many countries knew that Laplace had a good idea, but they also knew that if there was a standard meridian of longitude for the world, there would have to be a standard way of keeping time by the clock. All the clocks of the world should be made the same, and made so that the day would be divided into twenty-four equal parts, and then divided into minutes and seconds. This standard way of dividing up clock time would be figured out, just as it had been for hundreds of years, on the day of the equinox, when the day is divided by the sun into two equal parts from midday to midday. Someone went a step further and suggested that the Royal Observatory at Greenwich should be made the center of the timekeeping world. Scientists outside of England were willing to think about the idea, but nothing was done about it for several years.

Another problem map makers had to face was the different systems of measuring land that were used all over the world. Everyone, it seemed, used his own measuring stick, and there were very few that read the same. Map makers tried to get around the problem by telling their readers, on the map itself, just what scale of measure they had used. For example, on a single map of Turkey, the scale of measure was given in Turkish miles, Persian parasangs and English miles. On other maps and charts the scale was put down in Swiss leagues, French leagues and sea leagues. It was most confusing to anyone who tried to read a map printed in a foreign country. There was no one standard of measurement that everyone could understand. If an English map was drawn on a scale of one inch to an English mile, it meant something to Englishmen, but it did not mean much to a Russian or a German.

The problem of signs and symbols on maps was a bad one, and for a long time map makers did not know how to solve it. In 1880, there were more than a thousand different kinds of geographical features shown on maps, starting with cities and towns, roads, beaches, and rambling on through rivers, bridges and ferries. There were other symbols that represented orchards and vineyards, and still others that represented manufacturing centers and military installations. When it came to such important things as boundary lines, compass points and the slope of the land, every map maker had his own ideas. Map makers needed to get together.

The most troublesome problem of all was the spelling of place names, and notes to the reader — the language of the map. The map maker and reader of maps had to deal with several different alphabets and hundreds of different letters in order to understand the maps that were published in a foreign country. Maps were printed in Arabic, German, Greek, Hebrew, Russian, Chinese, Japanese and several other languages. All of these languages used strange letters in their alphabets, and even if a person knew the letters of the alphabet, he often had trouble deciding what the map maker was trying to say and the places he was trying to label. Should the name be written Moskva, Moscua, Moschia, Moscou, Moskau or Moscow? The ancient city of Lutetia or Lutetia Parisiorum might be correctly spelled Parigi in Italian, or Paris if you lived there, but what did the map world want, and how could map makers make themselves understood in any part of the world?

Map makers made a brave start. They did not lose hope, and one by one they solved the problems that would make it possible for the world to have an international map, a map which could be read and understood by everyone. One by one they established a universal prime meridian, a standard method of keeping time, a standard scale of measure, and a code of symbols and signs. The languages and alphabets of the world are still causing trouble, but map makers have not given up, and they are working every day towards the perfection of a map of the world for all men.

A standard system of measuring land came from the French, who developed and perfected the *metric* system of weights and measures. They did it for themselves, but most of the world has adopted it. What they wanted for a standard was a unit of measure which nature would provide, one that could be depended on, and one that would be small enough to handle without much trouble. They went to the Royal Academy of Sciences for advice, and found what they wanted. The scientists at the academy thought that the standard should be a small piece of the earth, a small section of the globe. It should be a section which could be divided into tenths, so that the arithmetic would be easy to figure. What they picked for a standard unit of measure was called a *meter,* and it was one forty-millionth part of the circumference of the globe.

The government of France was pleased with the idea of a metric system, and in 1798, after the French Revolution, there was a big celebration in Paris. Scientists from many

European nations came to celebrate a great event: the birth of a universal system of measure which every man could use. The standard itself was a bar of platinum one meter long, exactly. After the ceremony it was deposited in the National Archives of France, where it would be kept at a constant temperature and where the humidity would be controlled at all times.

Soon after the metric system was launched in France, geographers and map makers tried another scheme to describe the *scale* of a map. It was a "natural" or "fractional scale." One unit on the map was equal to X units on the ground, or "in nature." This new fractional scale (Representative Fraction, or R.F. scale) did not tell the whole story. It only stated that one unit of measure on the map was equal to just so many units of the earth's surface. And the unit might be anything. For this reason map makers had to add a little more information when they used the fractional scale, or Representative Fraction, as it is called today. They had to say that one inch on the map was equal to ten miles on the surface of the earth. Or they had to explain that they were using the French meter as a standard of measure, and that one meter on the map was equal to ten kilometers on the ground.

In 1871, right after the Franco-Prussian War had been settled, an International Congress of geographers was held at Antwerp. This gathering met to talk over the problems map makers would have to solve before an international map of the world could be finished. The delegates from all nations were invited to bring and exhibit maps and charts of all kinds, both historical and up to date, and several of them did. Nineteen countries were represented. Even if the delegates did not get much done, they at least got acquainted with one another, and before the meetings were over they all decided that they ought to talk some more. They wanted to decide what projection was the best one to use in making general maps and charts of the world. Would it be possible to make maps of the world with place names and labels that people in any country could understand? Would it be practical to establish a prime meridian for all the maps of the world? Was there an ice-free ocean at the North Pole? These were just a few of the questions that came up during the meetings.

The Third International Geographical Congress took place at Venice in 1881. By that time other countries had become interested in joining the discussions. Twenty-nine countries were represented. There were many handsome exhibits of maps and charts, and prizes were awarded for the best ones. When the serious talk started, the members of the Congress wanted to solve the problem of a prime meridian of longitude and fix a standard system of timekeeping. After many long discussions they decided there was a way to do both things at the same time. And the system would be simple.

In order to have a standard way of keeping time, they proposed to divide the earth just as the clock is divided — into twenty-four equal parts. But in this case the divisions would be meridians of longitude. These meridians would be spaced equally around the globe, fifteen degrees of longitude from one another, or one hour apart by the clock. Most of the delegates thought this was a good idea, but they all wanted to know which of the meridians was to be the prime meridian.

They studied their maps and discovered that the world could be cut in half from top to bottom, with twelve hours of clock time on each half. They could do this by using a meridian line through the Greenwich Observatory for one *standard* and a meridian line running down through the Bering Strait, halfway around the world, for the other line. Some of the delegates wanted the prime meridian to be fixed at the Bering Strait. But other members pointed out that, after all, it was half the way around the world. And, besides, you could not set up an observatory in the middle of the sea. After talking it over for many hours, the delegates decided that the business of having a standard system of keeping time was so important that a special meeting ought to be held to talk about nothing else.

No country in the world was more interested in a standard method of keeping time than the United States. Railroads had been built across the country from coast to coast, and time-keeping had become a serious problem. The northern boundary of the country between Canada and the United States is 3987 miles long, a span of 57 degrees of longitude. And because there was no standard system of timekeeping in the country, every railroad had its own system, and decided when to change the clock as their trains chugged across the country. Many a railroad station had three or four clocks, each one set according to a different time zone. And when two or three railroads used the same station, there might be a dozen clocks hung on the walls, each one keeping different time.

The President of the United States sent out invitations to all countries to send delegates to the First International Meridian Conference. Twenty-five countries sent delegates, and in October, 1884, they all sat down to settle the business of a prime meridian for all the world, and a standard way of keeping time. After the delegates had talked things over, they agreed on some important things. They chose the observatory at Greenwich, England, as the zero meridian of longitude, and they agreed that on all the maps their countries made, the meridians of longitude should be numbered from east and west of Greenwich, up to 180 degrees, or halfway around the world. They also decided that clock time should begin, for all the world, at the Greenwich Observatory. The standard day for the whole world was to begin at midnight at the Greenwich Observatory and hours of clock time were to be counted from there westward around the world from one to twenty-four.

Most countries were happy about this solution to two important problems. And most of them agreed that it would also be a good idea to divide the clock time around the world into twenty-four *belts* or *zones*, making each one fifteen degrees of longitude from the next one, or one hour apart. If this were done, international time, by the clock, would be reckoned according to the time zones as being so many hours east or west of Greenwich, until clock time was halfway around the world. From the day these decisions were made and accepted by most of the nations of the world, there have been a great many small adjustments made in the system of reckoning longitude and the keeping of time, but in most respects the standards which were fixed in Washington at the first Meridian Conference have remained unchanged. For the average citizen, however, time is still nothing more than the clock says, and that is enough. In general, the time kept by the town-hall clock or

202

the clock on the wall has been so well regulated by his government that even without a telescope or a sextant the sun always
seems to be high overhead at noon, and it most certainly cannot
be seen at midnight.

The science of cartography came of age in the 1890's, when,
for the first time in history, a group of men gathered together
to talk about making an international map of the world. The
event took place in Bern, Switzerland, and the year was 1890.
It was the Fifth International Geographical Congress. A young
man named Penck, a professor of geography at the University
of Vienna, stepped up to the platform and read to his fellow
scientists a plan for an international map of the world. All
nations would contribute to it, and all nations would be helped
by it. The map would be made on a scale of 1:1,000,000 (1M),
one inch being equal to 15.78 miles. The time and the audience
were right. The delegates listened and were interested.

Professor Penck had his troubles in Vienna. Most of the
people there agreed that the map was a good idea, but they
felt there were all kinds of details that would have to be
worked out, such as a map projection that would be most useful
to mankind. By the time the Eighth International Geographical
Congress met in Washington, in 1904, Professor Penck brought
along three trial maps that had been made in Europe, maps
that covered nearly 10,000,000 square miles. He showed the
delegates how these maps were drawn on a scale which could
be adjusted here and there to meet the standards of an international map. Professor Penck also begged the delegates from
North and South America to start work on this most important project, because, he said, the European traveler in the

United States usually had a hard time finding maps which would tell him how to get from place to place.

Work on the international map moved slowly, but it moved. Every year a few more countries were enlisted to co-operate on the project, and one by one the new sheets for the great map came rolling from the printing presses. At every International Conference a few more problems were solved and a few more differences of opinion were ironed out. Rules were established for signs and symbols as well as the spelling of place names. Color charts were sent out to all nations that were interested, so that the same tints would be used in every country to indicate such things as mountains and valleys. A Central Bureau for the Map was set up in Southampton, England, but before it was able to open for business World War I broke out. Work on the map came to a halt.

Years before, General Roy had said that the world has to be at peace in order to work on the surveying of a country or a great map of the world. But he also pointed out that wars make people move faster to turn out better maps. In wartime there are battles to be fought and won, and they cannot be won without maps. In 1913 the international map of the world was brushed aside, but map making did not stop in any country. Governments and their generals wanted maps in a hurry, and the maps and charts that were turned out for the military services were the best that could be had, but they were not made for neighboring countries to look at. They were secret documents.

In the United States there was a long pause in the progress of map making between World War I and World War II.

People forgot how important good maps and charts can be in peacetime as well as war. But just before World War II broke out, the United States government went to its map cupboard and found it was almost bare. And because there was a war just around the corner, every map-making department of the government got busy. It took a war to shake people up and make them remember that maps are the tools of warfare. But once the government in Washington realized how badly it needed better maps, not only maps of the United States but of all parts of the world, it moved fast.

Almost overnight the Army Map Service was organized, and in a few short years it became one of the most efficient map-making agencies in any country. It scoured the world for geographical information: maps, charts, photographs, paintings, and even diaries that told the Army and Navy the things they needed to know about the lands where the fighting was going on. Millions of map sheets were printed for the use of the armed forces and other departments of the government. Speed was almost more important than accuracy, and map makers took to the air, making aerial surveys that could be made into maps, because there was not time to make a survey on the ground. The progress made in the science of map making during the last war is a miracle that could never have happened in peacetime.

The United States, and many another country that took part in the last war, will never be caught napping again, because every thinking man and woman, every boy and girl, has learned an important lesson. People have learned that it is impossible to know a country well, to understand its social, its political and geographical problems without good maps. And everyone has learned that we cannot hope to have a world at peace and understand our neighbors unless we have world maps that every person can read and understand. But until the time when all men can sail up to a neighbor's shore without fear, and can ride or fly over any country without being shot at or stopped, the great map of the world that men have dreamed about for centuries must wait. Some day it may be finished.

Index

Kochab, 130

Lafreri, Antonio, atlas maker, 110
Laplace, Pierre Simon, 195
Lapland, 172
Latitude, first parallels of, 27, 28; science of, 119–132
Lewis, Meriwether, 186
Lewis and Clark expedition, 186
Libya, 60; deserts of, 75; cities of, 82
Line of Demarcation, 134–137
Little Dipper (Little Bear), 82, 128–131
Loadstone, 86
Local time, 143
London, map of, 180
Longitude, 133–165; at sea, 152–165; reward for finding, 154, 155; measurement of, 167; prime meridian of, 194–196
Louis XIV of France, 133, 147–149, 167
Louisiana Purchase, 183–186
Lully, Raymond, 130

Madeira Islands, 76
Magellan, Ferdinand, 134
Magnetite, 86
Malta, island of, 82
Maps, ancient, 3, 4; travelers', 4, 5; materials used in making, 5; secret, 5; Roman, 5, 6, 46, 47; of New World, 6; grid for, 7, 8, 36; clay, 26; Ptolemy's methods, 51; projections, 54, 93–96; decorations, 67; religious, 67–69; road, 73; Christian, 72; engraving, 100–118; coloring, 114–118; American, 182–190; language of, 198
Marco Polo, 72
Mars, the planet, 14, 15
Measure, linear, 196, 197
Mediterranean Sea, 67; Phoenicians sail it, 79–82; sailing directions for, 83
Mercator, Gerard, 91–96, 104, 106; projection, 91–96; portrait of, 111
Mercury, the planet, 15